NAIROBI
to
VANCOUVER

ERNEST W. LEFEVER, the founding president of the Ethics and Public Policy Center, has a B.D. and a Ph.D. in Christian ethics from Yale University. Among the books he has written are *Ethics and United States Foreign Policy* (1957 and 1986), *Nuclear Arms in the Third World* (1979), and *Amsterdam to Nairobi: The World Council of Churches and the Third World* (1979).

EDWARD NORMAN is the dean of Peterhouse college and a former lecturer in history at Cambridge University. He is an Anglican priest and has written widely on church history and on political ethics. His books include *Christianity and the World Order* (1979) and *The Victorian Christian Socialists* (1987).

NAIROBI
to
VANCOUVER

The World Council of Churches
and the World, 1975–87

Ernest W. Lefever

Foreword by Edward Norman

ETHICS AND PUBLIC POLICY CENTER

THE **ETHICS AND PUBLIC POLICY CENTER,** established in 1976, conducts a program of research, writing, publications, and conferences to encourage debate on domestic and foreign policy issues among religious, educational, academic, business, political, and other leaders. A nonpartisan effort, the Center is supported by contributions (which are tax deductible) from foundations, corporations, and individuals. The authors alone are responsible for the views expressed in Center publications. The founding president of the Center is **Ernest W. Lefever.**

Library of Congress Cataloging-in-Publication Data

Lefever, Ernest W.
Nairobi to Vancouver : the World Council of Churches and the world, 1975–87 / Ernest W. Lefever ; foreword by Edward Norman.
p. cm.
Bibliography: p.
Includes index.
1. World Council of Churches—Controversial literature.
2. Christianity and international affairs. I. World Council of Churches. II. Title
BX6.W78L44   1988
270.8′2′0601—dc 19   87–30302 CIP
ISBN 0–89633–117–2 (alk. paper)
ISBN 0–89633–118–0 (pbk. : alk. paper)

Distributed by arrangement with:
University Press of America, Inc.
4720 Boston Way
Lanham, MD 20706

3 Henrietta Street
London WC2E 8LU England

Ethics and Public Policy Center
1030 Fifteenth Street, N.W.
Washington, D.C. 20005
(202) 682-1200

For Paul Ramsey
Exacting Critic and Steadfast Friend

Contents

Foreword
By Edward Norman

IN RECENT CENTURIES, Christian believers have shown a persistent tendency to desert authentic spirituality for emotional and intellectual substitutes. Some of these substitutes have been recognizable variants of the faith, others have been aesthetic accomplishments or social ideologies. In our own day—and this will seem a paradox— the most common substitute is morality. Within the most informed Christian circles, and certainly within educated society in general, "religion" and "morality" are assumed to be virtually interchangeable terms. But they are actually very different things.

Christianity is an authentic religion because it speaks of the ultimate purposes of human existence, gives some insight into the mystery of the divine, and conveys, through the God who became man, forgiveness to men and women whose imperfection and corruption would otherwise convert human aspirations into empty rhetoric. Morality, on the other hand, is simply a code of reference that everyone uses; a moral code is either good or bad according to an external point of reference that may be quite arbitrarily determined.

In Christianity, that point of reference is fixed by God, so that, in the traditional language of theology, natural truth (morality) and revealed truth (spirituality) are seen in a proper balance, the one assisting the fulfillment of the other. Yet they remain distinct spheres of the Christian life. The modern tendency to identify Christianity with morality results in the progressive loosening of our spiritual moorings, a casting adrift of man's spiritual instinct. It is particularly hazardous when morality is defined in political terms.

Of all the international Christian agencies, the one that has most reflected this tendency to ethicize religion, and so to reduce the faith to one of its components, is the World Council of Churches. As Dr.

Ernest Lefever shows in this new study—a companion volume to his acclaimed *Amsterdam to Nairobi,* published in 1979—the WCC is not even balanced or professional in its chosen field of "moral" concern for peace, justice, and freedom. Its moral judgments are too selective, and its points of reference derive from worldly concerns. All too often anti-Christian ideologies are adopted virtually intact, without any acknowledgment of their patently alien qualities.

The problem begins in the several national councils of churches, particularly in the United States and western Europe. These bodies are unrepresentative of general Christian belief in their countries; they are led and governed by those whose educational level, leisure, middle-class lifestyle, and interest in current affairs draw them to such endeavors. The polemical edge—generally derived vicariously from the same fashionable sources that influence other members of the intellectual elites—is important. Given the continuing decay in authentic spirituality, the public issues they select—especially those related to military security, freedom, and poverty—engender passionate "involvement." This gives the participants a sense that what they call religion is at the center of the unfolding human drama.

In the international forum, this style of concern, equipped with a well-staffed bureaucracy, constitutes the WCC. Its periodic assemblies—six since its founding at Amsterdam in 1948—are ostensibly occasions for a cross-fertilization of Christian opinion. Increasingly, however, they have become celebrations of very similar and predictable viewpoints. The common bond of the WCC is evidently not a religious consensus but a shared social and political ideology, expressed in the fashionable language of secular thought and held with the closed mind that too often goes with "commitment."

Delegates to WCC assemblies from the Third World and from the Soviet bloc countries customarily express the political postulates of their own societies. Less through intimidation than through the human tendency to absorb prevailing ideals, the delegates from the "socialist" countries speak from a moral outlook and an agenda they share with their political elites. (The Catholic Church has been relatively more successful at resisting this tendency.) What is most distressing is the rush by WCC delegates from Western countries to associate themselves, and Christianity itself, with propaganda themes of the Soviet bloc. And what is true of the delegates at assemblies is equally true of the WCC's Central Committee, officers, and staff in Geneva.

Dr. Lefever's new book questions the very premises on which the

WCC operates and the process by which it selects issues to address. He lays bare the double standards that its officials regularly employ. In a work of notable precision, accuracy, and breadth of judgment, Dr. Lefever demonstrates exactly the kind of professionalism that the WCC and its votaries lack.

What is at stake in the modern world is freedom itself. Western liberalism is a potential victim of its own primary virtue—its openness to debate and criticism. This book, like its predecessor, focuses attention on the partiality and moral incoherence of an international body that ought to be, but is not, one of the most secure bastions of freedom.

Preface

On a bright blue day in Amsterdam in August 1948, more than a thousand Protestant leaders from the United States, Europe, Asia, Africa, and Latin America gathered in the Nieue Kerk, the Westminster of the Netherlands, for an ecumenical communion service. They were there to celebrate the founding of the World Council of Churches. Experiencing the mood of hope and expectation, one could not help being moved by this historic affirmation of Christian cooperation.

Seated next to me in the church was one of the few delegates from the Communist world, Professor Josef L. Hromádka, dean of the Jan Hus Theological Faculty at the University of Prague. Dr. Hromádka was also a member of the Central Action Committee of Czechoslovakia, which earlier that year had participated in the consolidation of Soviet control over his country.

During the colorful service, marked by liturgical elements from different traditions, Dr. Hromádka seemed troubled, as if he were torn by an inner struggle. I was soon to learn that he was indeed torn as he attempted to embrace both Marxism and Christianity and serve as a bridge between them. In a debate with John Foster Dulles, who represented the Presbyterian Church in the United States, Dr. Hromádka contended that the West had little moral or spiritual leadership to offer and that the churches must look to the East. He acknowledged that contemporary Communism did not fully respect the sacredness of the human person and the majesty of justice and love. But, he declared, Communism represents, "although under an atheistic form, much of the social impetus of the living church. . . . Many barbarians are, through the Communist movement, coming of age and aspiring to a place in the sun." The church, he said, must "make a new beginning, to start from the bottom and work for a new society, a new order" that will more adequately meet "the real needs of the present."

Little did I realize at the time that my companion in communion personified a struggle that within two decades would alter the character of the World Council of Churches and, perhaps more significantly, would manifest itself within the churches of all traditions throughout the world. It was a struggle between two radically opposed visions of Christian social and political responsibility.

At the opening session of the Amsterdam Assembly, Dr. W. A. Visser 't Hooft, the first general secretary of the Council, foreshadowed this struggle. Expressing regret at the refusal of the Russian Orthodox Church to send observers and its charge that the Council was primarily concerned "with gaining political and social influence," Dr. Visser 't Hooft said he remained hopeful because Moscow's negative stance was "based upon a complete misunderstanding of the true nature of our movement. . . . We should keep the door open for the church of Russia." The door was kept open, and in 1961 the Russian Orthodox Church became a full member of the Council.

The present volume grapples with the tensions and contradictions within the WCC personified by Dr. Hromádka at Amsterdam and later exacerbated by the active membership of the Russian Orthodox Church. Since this study covers the twelve years from the 1975 Council Assembly in Nairobi, Kenya, through mid-1987, it is both a sequel and a companion volume to my *Amsterdam to Nairobi: The World Council of Churches and the Third World,* which was published in 1979 and covers the first three decades of the WCC.

Amsterdam to Nairobi later appeared in both German and Korean editions. Many readers in America and abroad—especially after the 1983 WCC Assembly in Vancouver—urged me to update my analysis. This I have done. In undertaking the task, I have benefited from the encouragement, advice, and assistance of others.

First, I pay tribute to Paul Ramsey, whom I have known since 1950 and to whom this volume is affectionately dedicated. Dr. Ramsey is emeritus professor of Christian ethics at Princeton University. He has written many books, taught many students, and made many speeches. But he has done a great deal more. He has made a seminal contribution to Christian moral theology in our time. His book *The Just War: Force and Political Responsibility* (1968) is a classic. Paul Ramsey's critique of the Protestant ecumenical "social witness" is more trenchant than that of any other contemporary theologian. These troubled times would be less troubled if more scholars and statesmen read and understood the wisdom of Paul Ramsey.

Turning to those who have assisted me directly, I express a special debt to J. A. Emerson Vermaat, a Dutch journalist-scholar, who wrote a comprehensive analytical account of selected international issues addressed by the WCC since 1975. I drew upon his manuscript in the early stages of this study. *Nairobi to Vancouver,* which relies heavily on official Council documents, has been enriched by Mr. Vermaat's first-hand reports of Central Committee meetings and of the Assemblies at Nairobi in 1975 and Vancouver in 1983. Mr. Vermaat studied law at the University of Leiden, where he also teaches. His reporting appears frequently in European papers, and his articles have been published in academic journals in Europe and the United States.

Six of the issue chapters were improved by the editorial work of Patricia Buckley Bozell. The study also benefited from the comments of several outside critics, including Thomas S. Derr and Kent Hill.

Within the Ethics and Public Policy Center staff, I was fortunate to have the assistance and support of Robert Royal, vice president for research; Carol Griffith, editor; David A. Bovenizer, associate editor, who ably bore the burden of verifying elusive facts and sources; research assistants Michael Mazarr and Robert Vander Lugt; and my secretary, Susan Pierce.

I alone am responsible for the facts selected, the analysis, and the conclusions in the pages that follow.

ERNEST W. LEFEVER, *President*
Ethics and Public Policy Center

August 1987

CHAPTER ONE

The World Council
and the World

IN MID-1983 the world was replete with its normal quota of anxiety and suffering—poverty, famine, tyranny, local wars, terrorism, regional conflict, the nuclear arms standoff between the superpowers, and an expanding Soviet empire. Three million Afghan refugees had fled to Pakistan and Iran to escape the brutal Soviet occupation of their homeland. Hundreds of thousands of Ethiopians had died from starvation and forced migration. The Sandinista regime in Nicaragua had expelled thousands of Indians and was tightening its grip over all areas of political, economic, and religious life. Twenty-five thousand Cuban troops upheld a minority Marxist regime in Angola, a country that saw the heaviest fighting between government forces and Angolan freedom fighters since the mid-1970s.

In Poland, riot police had broken up large, nationwide pro-Solidarity demonstrations. Germany and Korea remained divided, and the Berlin Wall was still intact. Vietnam had been united by a war of aggression and was living under a Soviet-backed regime that had produced hundreds of thousands of "boat people" and was engaged in armed attacks against Kampuchea and refugee camps on the Thai border. Libya was continuing its destabilization campaign against neighboring Chad.

In every case, the tragedy reflected the perennial conflict between the drive for power and human dignity, and in most cases there was an actual or potential clash between two profoundly different ways of organizing society—government based on consent and government based on coercion.

The United States, for its part, was still suffering from its 1975 defeat in Vietnam. Though an unquestioned superpower and the leader of the

1

Free World, Washington's responses to thrusts of Soviet power and to chaos and poverty in the Third World were often uncertain and inadequate. The United States had not yet shaken off the shroud of self-doubt and continued to chafe under the burdens of power that history had thrust upon it.

America also faced internal economic, political, and social problems rooted in the counterculture and radicalism of the 1960s and 1970s that continued to have a corrosive effect on the family, religious institutions, and the academy. America had many flaws, but a drive to impose its will on other peoples was not one of them. We were in the partial grip of a new isolationism that made it difficult to support adequately the disciplines of foreign policy and national defense. To be sure, NATO and our other alliances were still intact, but allies and friends around the world wondered, often out loud, whether the American people had the will to act like a humane superpower.

It was to this turbulent, conflicted, and suffering world that the Sixth Assembly of the World Council of Churches, meeting in Vancouver, Canada, July 24–August 10, 1983, addressed its Christian concern, its analysis, and its prescription for justice and peace. Thirty-five years had passed since the founding Assembly of the Council in Amsterdam in 1948, and the last Assembly before Vancouver was held in Nairobi, Kenya, in 1975. At Vancouver, 847 voting delegates grappled with broad issues such as Christian unity, evangelism, and what they chose to call "world affairs in ecumenical perspective." That perspective, as we shall see, was selective, and usually focused on issues in which Western views and interests conflicted with the views and interests of the Marxist world, particularly the Soviet Union.

To a significant extent the Assembly's advice on world affairs reflected the origin of the delegates. The regional distribution was: North America, 158; Western Europe, 152; the Soviet Union and Eastern Europe, 142; Africa, 131; Asia, 114; Middle East, 53; Latin America, 30; Caribbean, 19; Australia and New Zealand, 26; and the Pacific, 22. In political terms, the 336 delegates from Western countries (including Australia and New Zealand) were outnumbered by the 511 from the Soviet bloc and Third World.[1] Soviet bloc delegates tended to support the views of their governments; those from the Third World generally reflected either their government's views or those of the intellectual elite. In the democratic West, many delegates supported positions highly critical of their governments.

Afghanistan and Central America—Examples

The Vancouver Assembly's resolutions on the continuing tragedy in Afghanistan and the Central American conflict may be cited briefly to illustrate the interest and orientation of the World Council of Churches on the wider range of international issues discussed in this study. In December 1979, Soviet armed forces had invaded Moslem Afghanistan at the "request" of the Moscow-installed regime in Kabul. As of early 1987, some 120,000 Soviet troops armed with tanks, helicopter gunships, personnel carriers, and many other weapons were still fighting the Afghan resistance, though Moscow had begun making proposals for a ceasefire. In addition, there were some 9,000 Soviet civilians working in Afghanistan. By all independent accounts, the Soviet occupation has been one of the most brutal of this bloody century. The Red Army, for example, deployed booby traps in the form of small mines disguised as toys and designed to maim, but not kill. A child without hands or feet is a greater burden to resisting villagers than a dead child. Claude Malhuret, executive director of Médecins sans Frontières, a Paris-based medical relief organization working in Afghanistan, noted this point in 1984: "Camouflaged anti-personnel mines are not designed to kill, but to injure. The Russians know quite well that in this type of war, an injured person is much more trouble than a dead person. The injured person demobilizes fighters who have to transport him. . . . Damage [is] caused by the explosion of booby-trapped toys, in most cases plastic pens or small red trucks, which are choice terror weapons. Their main targets are children, whose hands and arms are blown off. It is impossible to imagine any objective that is more removed from conventional military strategy, which forswears civilian targets."[2]

To any unprejudiced eye the basic situation was clear. The Soviet Union was and still is seeking to extend its empire southward by brute force, and the democratic West is trying, albeit halfheartedly, to prevent Afghanistan from becoming a full-fledged Soviet client state. Through Pakistan the United States has provided arms and humanitarian aid to the Afghans defending their homeland. Along with several other Western countries and international organizations, Washington has called for the withdrawal of all Soviet troops, but Moscow first wants a political settlement that includes the end of "imperialist" (read U.S.) assistance to the freedom fighters.

Neither the WCC Vancouver Assembly staff (168 members of the

WCC staff, plus 194 temporary staff including interpreters and translators) nor the delegates could dodge this dramatic and divisive issue. After parliamentary maneuvering and debate in which some delegates called for "a condemnation of Soviet aggression and the unconditional withdrawal of Soviet troops," a compromise resolution was adopted.[3] The final statement acknowledged that "continued fighting" has caused "tremendous suffering," but it did not mention the Soviet invasion nor identify the cause of the suffering. It said Soviet troops should be withdrawn "in the context of an overall political settlement, including agreement between Afghanistan and the USSR," that is, between Moscow and its Soviet-imposed regime in Kabul. It called for "an end to the supply of arms to the opposition groups from outside," meaning that military supplies to the freedom fighters, primarily from the United States, should cease.

The Russian Orthodox Church called the final resolution "balanced and realistic." WCC General Secretary Philip Potter agreed. Many voices in the religious and secular press were outraged by what they saw as capitulation by an international ecumenical body to the Soviet position on Afghanistan. (This issue is elaborated in Chapter 4. See also Appendix A.)

Moving from the Soviet sphere of influence in Asia to the U.S. sphere of influence in Central America, the Vancouver Assembly turned its attention to Nicaragua and El Salvador. By 1983 the Sandinista Marxist regime in Managua had heavily censored the press, intimidated the political opposition, tortured prisoners, forcibly uprooted the Miskito Indians, publicly insulted Pope John Paul II, and arrested uncooperative Catholic priests and Moravian ministers. Despite this systematic repression, the Assembly found little or no fault with the regime and supported the small, unrepresentative "popular church" that backed the Sandinistas. The Council excused Managua's forced relocation of the Miskito Indians, though in 1982 the WCC Central Committee had condemned the United States, Canada, New Zealand, Australia, Brazil, Chile, Colombia, Guatemala, Mexico, and the Philippines, but *not* Nicaragua, for mistreating "indigenous peoples."

The Vancouver Assembly found "promising signs of life" in Marxist Nicaragua, but not in El Salvador, where in a 1982 national election 70 percent of the voters turned out despite guerrilla harassment. Its Central American resolution repeatedly portrayed the United States as the only external aggressive, militaristic, and repressive force in the region. U.S. "military, economic, financial, and political initiatives" were "designed to destabilize the Nicaraguan government, renew international support for Guatemala's violent military regimes, resist the forces of historic change in El Salvador, and militarize Honduras in order to contain the aspirations of the Central American peoples" and to prevent the "export of revolution."[4]

The resolution praised the "life-affirming achievements of the Nicaraguan people and its leadership" since the Sandinistas came to power in 1979. There was no mention of Cuba or the Soviet Union, both of whom maintained a massive military and intelligence presence in Nicaragua, nor of Managua's insistence on pursuing a Marxist "revolution without borders." Respected scholars on Central American affairs could discern no difference in the WCC resolution and the views espoused by Moscow and Havana. The WCC's pronouncements on Central America are elaborated in Chapter 3. (See also Appendix B.)

For Whom Does the WCC Speak?

The position of the Vancouver Assembly on Afghanistan and Central America angered many church members whose denominations belonged to the WCC. They regarded the Council's stance as one-sided if not outright pro-Soviet. Broad criticism was also voiced in the secular press. How could a body dedicated to Christian unity become so lopsided and divisive? How could Christian churches motivated by a gospel of love, peace, freedom, and compassion overlook the brutality of the Soviet Union in Afghanistan or the repressiveness of the Sandinista regime in Nicaragua? Why was the WCC more consistently critical of the United States than of the Soviet Union?

This modest study will attempt to answer these questions, first by identifying a yardstick for judging WCC statements and examining briefly what the Council is and how it makes decisions. The study will then trace specific pronouncements on international questions from the Fifth Assembly in Nairobi in 1975, through early 1987, with particular emphasis on the Vancouver Assembly in 1983.

This book is both a sequel and companion volume to my study, *Amsterdam to Nairobi: The World Council of Churches and the Third World,* published in 1979 by the Ethics and Public Policy Center. The earlier work focuses on the WCC's approach to Asia, Africa, and Latin America, and covers the three decades from 1948 to 1978. The present volume addresses a larger range of international issues and covers the twelve years since the Nairobi Assembly in 1975. There is a deliberate overlap of three years to provide connective tissue and perspective. Both books deal with an institution that has changed little since 1975. Hence, my concluding observations remain similar to those of 1979. Chapters two through eight focus on the WCC's views in seven major areas.

A Yardstick for Judging Council Views

Both studies are based on a fundamental premise shared by the great majority of contemporary Christians—mainline Protestants, evangelicals, and Catholics—that Christians as individuals and the churches as corporate bodies have a responsibility to speak to this world. Believers may disagree sharply on the nature of that responsibility and how it should be carried out, but they acknowledge that Christian bodies have an obligation to speak out against egregious evils and to participate in the debate on all consequential moral issues. This speaking out—whether in sermons, articles, educational materials, or formal pronouncements—should above all be responsible. Church pronouncements must be morally grounded and empirically informed to be politically relevant. Unfortunately, there is no single and agreed upon Christian social tradition that can serve as a universal and absolute guide. There is no easy-to-apply moral yardstick in a complex world.

Several streams of Christian thought emphasize the other-worldly dimension of the Christian faith—personal salvation and preparation for the next world—over the concerns of this world. The traditions that acknowledge the necessity for a "social gospel" fall into two principal schools: one stresses continuity, orderly change, and reform; the other, radical discontinuity and revolutionary change. Advocates of both schools seek justice, freedom, security, and peace, but they differ on which objective should take precedence in particular circumstances and what means should be used to achieve these ends.

Christians also divide over what can reasonably be expected from human nature and what can be achieved in this world. Some believe in the perfectibility of man and the possibility, if not the inevitability, of progress within history. Others place greater emphasis on original sin;

hence they expect less from human nature and history and strive for more limited political and social goals.

The central Christian tradition has insisted that under no circumstances should any church or Christian body identify itself fully with any specific secular cause or order, whether a prevailing political or economic system or challenges to it. In identifying with a secular power or movement, the church risks losing its critical distance and subverting its prophetic function—its capacity to judge all movements and systems by its universal standards.

The yardstick for evaluating the Council's views on international issues in this volume is rooted in the classic Christian moral tradition as expressed in 1948 by the founding Assembly of the WCC in Amsterdam in its basic report, *The Church and the Disorder of Society*. (See Appendix C.) "Christians are conscious of the sins which corrupt human communities and institutions in every age" and of "the perennial evil in human history," but they must seek, the report stated, to "overcome" or "control" specific social, economic, and political disorders. The statement continued:

Men are often disillusioned by finding that changes of particular systems do not bring unqualified good, but fresh evils. New temptations to greed and power arise even in systems more just than those they have replaced because sin is ever present in the human heart. Many, therefore, lapse into apathy, irresponsibility and despair. The Christian faith leaves no room for such despair, being based on the fact that the Kingdom of God is firmly established in Christ and will come by God's act despite all human failure.

This sober assessment of human nature and history reflects the mainstream of Christian thought since biblical times and has been voiced by recent American Protestant theologians such as Reinhold Niebuhr, Paul Ramsey, and Carl F. H. Henry, and by Catholic theologians such as John Courtney Murray, S. J. These men can be described as morally concerned realists in their approach to public issues. They and the Amsterdam statement reject all forms of religious and secular utopianism.[5] This non-utopian view stands in marked contrast to the comparable WCC document produced by the Nairobi Assembly in 1975. Several brief quotations from the latter will make the point.

The 1975 report on *Structures of Injustice and Struggles for Liberation* (Appendix D carries the full text) embraces a mixture of religious and secular utopianism. It assumes that man can be liberated from the "structures of injustice" and "other destructive powers," but does not acknowledge clearly that the new liberated order will be subject to further injustice or corruption. Evil appears to reside exclusively in external forces rather than in the human heart. Liberation requires, for example, that the grip of unspecified Western "governments and power systems" on the Third World countries be broken.

Another unjust structure to be eliminated is racism, particularly white racism that is fed by capitalism and "trade patterns" created by "predominantly white North American nations" to discriminate "against other racial groups" and to support "racist regimes." The Assembly condemned all forms of racism, but focused almost exclusively on the "self-serving policies of transnational corporations" that "operate across boundaries with impunity" and provide "weapons and mercenaries" to "local elites." The churches were urged to invoke sanctions against South Africa and help to alleviate the "condition of the native peoples" of North and South America, Australia, and New Zealand.

How the WCC Operates

The declared objective of the World Council of Churches is to develop greater Christian unity among the various denominations and to mount an effective social witness. After a decade of planning, interrupted by World War II, the Council was created in Amsterdam in August 1948. At that time there were 152 member denominations from forty-six countries. By 1986 the WCC had grown to 305 member churches from over 100 countries.

The WCC emerged from six international Christian conferences that since 1910 had dealt with two main streams of Christian concern. The *Faith and Order* stream has focused on doctrinal and ecclesiastical questions, and on promoting the Christian faith around the world, while *Life and Work* has emphasized the application of Christianity to social, political, and economic problems. Within the WCC, *Life and Work* later came to be called *Church and Society*. The interplay between the two major emphases can be seen in the evolving responses of the Council to international issues.

As in any large, bureaucratic organization, the decisions of the WCC emerge from a complex but generally orderly process. The Council speaks with words and deeds when it addresses world problems. Its words have varying degrees of authority, depending on the issuing agency. When it speaks with deeds—and this usually means with money—the full authority of the organization stands behind it.

The highest authoritative body of the WCC is the Assembly, which meets every six to eight years. There have been six:

1. Amsterdam, Holland, 1948
2. Evanston, Illinois, 1954
3. New Delhi, India, 1961
4. Uppsala, Sweden, 1968
5. Nairobi, Kenya, 1975
6. Vancouver, Canada, 1983

The seventh Assembly is scheduled for Canberra, Australia, in 1990, with the theme: "Justice, Peace, and the Integrity of Creation."

These Assemblies make the major decision on the character and direction of the WCC's work. They include delegates from all member churches, apportioned roughly according to size; the Vancouver Assembly had 847 delegates. Between Assemblies, the authoritative agency is the Central Committee, consisting of approximately 135 members elected by the Assembly. In January 1987, the WCC held its thirty-eighth Central Committee meeting. In the current Committee, as in 1975, representatives from Third World and Marxist states together outnumber those from Western states. Between Central Committee meetings, its Executive Committee of twenty-five to thirty members acts on its behalf.

Four other elements of the World Council also exercise a policymaking role: (1) its seven concurrent presidents from different geographical regions and ecclesiastic traditions; (2) special standing bodies, such as the Commission of the Churches on International Affairs and the Program to Combat Racism; (3) WCC-sponsored study groups and larger meetings, such as the World Conference on Church and Society, held in Geneva in 1966, that serve as program catalysts for the official bodies; and (4) the secretariat of the Geneva headquarters, which serves all elements of the WCC and plays a major role in setting the Council agenda. As of February 1987, the staff numbered approximately 275.

During the 1975–1987 period the WCC had two general secretaries. The Rev. Dr. Philip Potter, a clergyman of the Methodist Church of the Caribbean and the Americas in Dominica, served from 1972 to

1985. The Rev. Dr. Emilio Castro, a clergyman of the Evangelical Methodist Church in Uruguay, has served since January 1985. The WCC maintains an office, with a staff of five, in New York City, located in the Interchurch Center at 475 Riverside Drive. The Center also houses the U.S. National Council of Churches and many headquarters offices of denominations affiliated with both councils.

The WCC operates formally by Western parliamentary procedures.[6] Each delegate to an Assembly and each member of the Central Committee has one vote, and questions are decided by majority rule. The WCC headquarters staff in Geneva, Switzerland, plays a highly influential role because it determines the agenda for discussion, develops project proposals, plans conferences and proposes conference themes, commissions preparatory materials and selects authors, employs consultants, and generally utilizes the full range of assets available to the senior staff in any large organization.

The different levels of authority and degrees of consensus with which the WCC speaks are largely lost on most church members and the general public. An Assembly or the Central Committee may simply *receive* a report from a study group or special committee and commend it to the churches, or it may *adopt* the report as a policy statement. In addressing international issues, the Executive Committee may act in its own name, or the seven WCC presidents may act in theirs. In certain situations, the WCC's general secretary may speak in his own name.

In practice, these levels of authority are not as significant as they may appear to be because of the substantial degree of consensus that exists among the statements issued by the various WCC units, a consensus rooted in a similarity of outlook among the senior staff in Geneva and the various elected bodies with whom they work. Though there are differences, a largely predictable stance has developed over the years because of a kind of likeminded self-selection among WCC activists—a phenomenon noted in 1967 by Paul Ramsey.[7]

Questions to Be Addressed

The operation and program of the WCC raise several crucial questions: *For* whom does the WCC speak? Does it speak and act for the member churches? Or does it speak and act only for itself? And *to* whom does it speak? Does it speak only to the churches and individual Christians, or also to governments and the world?

It takes no sophisticated analysis to recognize that only in a vague, symbolic, and incomplete sense does the WCC speak *for* all its member churches. As a matter of fact, it speaks for none of them, a point made by the late Archbishop William Temple, a major architect of the pre-WCC ecumenical movement, as early as 1938. And it certainly can never speak for the millions of believers of its member churches, much less for all Christians. Its pronouncements are *addressed to* the churches and to individual Christians, as well as to the world—more specifically, to particular governments or agencies whose behavior it seeks to encourage, modify, or condemn.

Does the WCC, or any particular denomination for that matter, have the right to take a position that runs counter to the majority views of its members? Clearly, many WCC political pronouncements contradict the majority opinion within some if not most of its member churches. Does this mean that these pronouncements lack authority? The usual reply is that the WCC should make a "prophetic witness" rather than reflect a current consensus, and that pronouncements should not hesitate to condemn the status quo or call for reform or radical change—even if most church members continue to oppose the position being advanced. There is merit to this position. Indeed, the moral authority or political wisdom of a statement, according to this view, derives from its intrinsic quality rather than from consensus. Consequently, church members, the public generally, and governments to whom pronouncements are addressed should recognize that any wisdom, foolishness, or error in a particular statement should *not* be attributed to the millions of Christians in whose name the WCC seems to speak. The millions of church members who are dissatisfied with WCC pronouncements should exercise all the democratic means at their disposal to see that the Council takes seriously the full range of views and experience represented among them. To do less is to yield to the radical activists who have dominated the WCC since the mid-1960s.

Criticism has also been directed against the WCC for making pronouncements on specific issues without adequately examining the relevant underlying theological and ethical principles. And it has been faulted by Paul Ramsey and others for frequently ignoring the most reliable empirical information available on the issue under consideration, and turning, instead, to the diagnosis and prescriptions of secular ideologies, including those heavily influenced by Marxism.[8]

The following pages seek to shed further light on these matters. The ensuing chapters will focus on the WCC's treatment of seven international issues: (2) nuclear arms, (3) Central America, (4) Afghanistan, (5) southern Africa, (6) East Asia and the Pacific, (7) the economic question, and (8) religion in the Soviet bloc.

The problem of ascertaining the WCC's position on any of these issues was often difficult. I was primarily interested in identifying the operational policy advice on specific international issues, whether addressed to individual Christians, churches, governments, or other audiences. Occasionally I had to infer what the specific advice was, or to whom it was directed, because the statements were often vague and haphazard, lacking a clear connection between the ostensible premises and the explicit advice.

Most of the pronouncements contained little historical background either in moral theology or in the concrete international problem being addressed. In this respect WCC statements were far inferior to papal encyclicals and to pronouncements and reports of the U.S. Catholic bishops, which are more carefully researched and crafted. WCC statements were also far less adequate than the best secular academic or journalistic analyses of the same issues.

A closely related problem in presenting a coherent presentation and analysis of WCC views is that Council bodies did not address the issues in a systematic, comprehensive, or coherent way. To a considerable extent, the drafters, frequently the Council staff, were prompted by recent headlines, prevailing propaganda slogans, or secular political movements. This was particularly true of the statements on nuclear arms, in which there was little evidence of any substantial understanding of the solid literature in this complex area.

This hit-and-miss approach that Paul Ramsey called "leapfrogging from one problem to another"[9] often neglected central issues, notably those arising from the struggle between totalitarian and democratic systems, and focused on peripheral fragments of the rich tapestry of international politics. Further, the statements were often hurriedly drafted and attempted unsuccessfully to reconcile diverse views. The reader should take into account these problems as I attempt to present the material in a rational and systematic way.

The last two chapters evaluate the WCC's behavior in the international arena in the light of the Christian moral tradition as well as by the political relevance and probable consequences of its activity. The epilogue addresses the WCC's future prospects.

CHAPTER TWO

Nuclear Arms

FROM THE DAY THAT Hiroshima was destroyed by an American atomic bomb, Christians and many others have sought to control or eliminate nuclear weapons. The topic was addressed by the World Council of Churches Assembly in Evanston, Illinois, in 1954[1] and many times by the WCC's Commission of the Churches on International Affairs. But it was not until 1979 that the Council formally established a special Program for Disarmament and Against Militarism and the Arms Race. This effort was patterned after the WCC Program to Combat Racism. Churches from the Soviet bloc, especially those from the USSR and Hungary, supported this initiative, as did the Prague-based Christian Peace Conference (CPC), which attempted to set the tone for the WCC's Nairobi Assembly in 1975 with the statement that "strivings for the survival of humanity represent a practical ecumenism."[2]

At a WCC Consultation on Militarism held in Glion, Switzerland, in November 1977, disarmament was joined to the struggle for justice: "military forces today in both developed and developing societies sustain and promote unjust economic, social, and political structures." The report spoke of "the competition of the two superpowers to gain . . . superiority" and warned that development of first strike capabilities would "bring us even nearer to the brink of a new world war." Finally, it condemned "the frequently used argument of national security" as "no justification for this arms race."[3]

The conclusions of this and other WCC conferences do not carry the authority of formal pronouncements, but they do find their way into resolutions of the Central Committee, in part because WCC staff and others are involved in both. One of the most ardent supporters of the Disarmament Program was Alexei Buevski, a secretary of the Moscow Patriarchate of the Russian Orthodox Church and a veteran of WCC Central Committee meetings.

13

Because the WCC tends to link militarism, capitalism, and the profit motive, the Council placed the primary blame for the internationa arms race on Western democratic countries. Accordingly, the 197 Glion meeting spoke of "a coalition between the military commandin the means of violence and the existing social and economic order, and again, "the rise of the 'military-industrial complex' in industria ized and developed countries, particularly where the profit motive active."[4] This formulation targets the United States and its NAT partners and overlooks the larger and far more centrally controlle military–industrial–Communist Party complex in the Soviet Union.

The WCC returned to Glion in April 1978 to prepare for the Unite Nations' First Special Session on Disarmament scheduled for later tha year. The Council declared that "it is the prophetic duty of Christian to unmask and challenge idols of military doctrine and technology ir the light of the Christian vision of justice and peace." A primary idol the Council made clear, is "the doctrine of deterrence which holds millions hostage to the threat of nuclear terror." This meeting reiterated the "clear relationship between the armaments race and socioeconomic order," implying that capitalism was a chief cause of militarism.[5]

NATO's Nuclear Defense

In December 1979, the NATO governments approved the deployment in Europe of 464 Tomahawk cruise missiles and 108 Pershing II ballistic missiles to counter the rapidly growing arsenal of the more powerful and longer-range Soviet SS-20 missiles targeted against cities and military installations from Norway to Turkey. The deployment was linked to proposed negotiations for arms control to establish "agreed limitations on U.S. and Soviet-based long-range theater nuclear missile systems."[6]

The WCC immediately expressed "serious concern" over the NATO deployment.[7] By August 1980, the Central Committee was convinced that "the hands of the clock have moved closer to the midnight of nuclear war." The Council warned of the increased tension between the United States and the Soviet Union, "heightened by the NATO decision to base new missiles."

Full censure by the Central Committee finally fell on NATO, and NATO alone. An earlier, more evenhanded draft had observed that

"the United States and the Soviet Union seem to be ready to apply a nuclear war-fighting strategy."[8] But the Committee repeatedly gave in to the views of Soviet delegate Buevski and altered the text. The final version went so far as to suggest that the United States and NATO were actually contemplating "limited nuclear war."[9]

Pressure from Soviet bloc church representatives gained momentum at the August 1981 Central Committee meeting in Dresden, East Germany. Their greatest victory was the Committee's long statement on "Increased Threats to Peace and the Tasks for the Churches." The Committee sharply denounced "new dehumanizing weapons" like the U.S. neutron bomb, which was termed "a tremendous threat because it makes the use of nuclear weapons more likely" and was deemed "a further incentive to escalate the arms race." The Council failed to note that the "neutron bomb" was more humane than the weapons it was to replace. There was no reference to larger, more destructive Soviet theater weapons, the near-monopoly of Warsaw Pact forces in short-range nuclear missiles, or the three-to-one superiority the Soviets held over NATO in conventional tanks.

The statement called on churches around the world to challenge "military and militaristic policies," to stop "the trend to characterize those of other nations and ideologies as 'the enemy' through the promotion of hatred and prejudice," and, finally, to "assist in de-mythologizing current doctrines of national security."[10]

Deterrence and Disarmament

In late 1981, the WCC held an International Hearing on Nuclear Weapons and Disarmament in Amsterdam attended by theological, political, and military leaders and representatives of several peace movements. The visitors were asked to speak before a carefully selected "Hearing Group" that included church leaders with strong ties to the Soviet-sponsored Christian Peace Conference, such as Bishop Karoly Toth of Hungary and Metropolitan Paulos Gregorios of India. Peace Conference participants include many Christian pacifists and others who do not accept Marxism, but believe that a Marxist-Christian dialogue can strengthen the cause of peace.

Not surprisingly, the peace groups pressed for, and won, an across-the-board condemnation of the doctrine of nuclear deterrence and the possession of nuclear arms. The statement claimed that "the strategy

of nuclear deterrence, and the weapons on which it depends, are as unmitigated an evil as an actual nuclear war," and, moreover, "the possession of such weapons and the readiness to use them are wrong in the sight of God and should be treated as such by the churches."[11]

At the hearing, the churches were urged to declare unequivocally that "the production and deployment as well as the use of nuclear weapons are a crime against humanity" and "must be condemned on ethical and theological grounds."[12] The WCC later officially adopted these views. This statement in principle applied to all nuclear powers, but other WCC pronouncements and spokesmen made it clear that the U.S. policy of deterrence was the chief target.

As an alternative to nuclear deterrence ("a new form of idolatry"), the Amsterdam delegates urged "common security," a policy whereby governments would assure their national security by cooperating with their adversaries.[13] This proposal was developed by Egon Bahr, a German Social Democrat, and Georgi Arbatov, a personal advisor to Soviet leader Leonid Brezhnev.

During the Amsterdam deliberations, vital distinctions between East and West were repeatedly blurred. The opening remarks by the Rev. William Sloane Coffin, Jr., anticipated the mood of the entire proceedings: "Were we truly to hear Jesus' words . . . Soviet threats to rebellious Poles would call to mind American threats to rebels in El Salvador; and Afghanistan would prompt us to remember Vietnam."[14] This was not the first time that the senior minister of New York's Riverside Church invoked the myth of moral symmetry to condemn U.S. policies.

In 1982, the Central Committee endorsed the Amsterdam findings, emphasizing that "the production and deployment, as well as the use, of nuclear weapons are a crime against humanity."[15]

The Central Committee also "received with appreciation" a Program for Disarmament and Against the Arms Race report that sought to broaden the disarmament issue from its East-versus-West confines. The Disarmament Program insisted that "not only militarism and the arms race, but also social injustice, economic deprivation, political repression, and environmental devastation have to be exposed."[16]

Militarism and Economic Injustice

The 1983 Vancouver Assembly had more of the same to say about peace and national security. A West German invited advisor, Dorothee

Soelle, struck a responsive chord when she charged that the West is "under the domination of NATO" and denounced militarism as "humanity's supreme effort to get rid of God once and for all."[17] A prominent group at the Assembly took it from there. The group, "Confronting Threats to Peace and Survival," chaired by Paulos Gregorios of India, said that the strategic doctrine of nuclear deterrence, a cornerstone of U.S. and NATO defense policy, is "morally unacceptable because it relies on the credibility of the intention to use nuclear weapons," and urged that the doctrine be "categorically rejected as contrary to our faith in Jesus Christ."[18]

The group also espoused the Amsterdam "common security" solution, saying that only "a common enterprise undertaken by all the nations of the world together can ensure dependable international security. . . . Deterrence or peace by terror should give place to the concept of common security for all."[19] The report also acknowledged that "deterrence provides an interim assurance of peace and stability." Pope John Paul II, after all, had declared that nuclear deterrence may be judged morally acceptable if considered "as a step on the way to progressive disarmament."[20]

The Vancouver Assembly statement "Justice, Peace and Militarism" reflected past WCC themes and underscored the alleged relationship between militarism and economic injustice. It asserted that "the present military build-up and arms race are integrally related to the practices of an unjust world economic order" and that militarism is advanced by technology, "growing integration of military and civilian sectors, a conscious promotion of psychological insecurity," an "alarming increase in the number of foreign military bases," and an "unhealthy competition between the USA and the USSR to achieve military and technological superiority."[21] It was not clear whether the drafters were expressing a moral symmetry between Washington and Moscow, or were placing the burden of blame on the United States. In another section on "rampant militarism," the Assembly sought to demythologize "current doctrines of national security and elaborate new concepts of security based on justice and the rights of the peoples" and asserted that "economic injustice, oppression and exploitation" were "the root causes of war."[22] Terms like "social and economic injustice" are frequently used by the Soviet Union to evade the issue at hand by condemning the West for unemployment, poverty, oppression, and militarism.

In its comprehensive statement on nuclear disarmament, the Central

Committee, at a meeting in Geneva in January 1987 (the third since the Vancouver Assembly), reaffirmed earlier WCC positions and added some new specifics. It opposed nuclear war and rejected nuclear deterrence, but admitted that "conventional weapons" have "claimed the lives of many more people than have nuclear weapons. In addition, the increasing sophistication of conventional weapons almost blurs the distinction between non-nuclear and nuclear weapons."[23]

The committee saw "new opportunities" for disarmament and peace, along with continuing anxieties. It urged three "immediate steps": a comprehensive test ban treaty, an end to production of all types of nuclear arms, and a phased plan for a "progressive and balanced reduction" of nuclear stockpiles and their means of delivery.

The signs of hope sensed by the Committee included the "many peace movements," the "principled opposition of governments like New Zealand to nuclear weapons," and initiatives such as "the South Pacific Forum for Nuclear-Free Zone Treaties." It said that the 1986 Reykjavik Summit between President Reagan and Chairman Gorbachev had demonstrated that "nuclear disarmament is possible," but noted there was no agreement on America's Strategic Defense Initiative.

The Committee appealed to Washington and Moscow to stop nuclear tests, eliminate medium range missiles, and "prevent the development of space weapons," policies already publicly urged by the Soviet Union. It appealed to the "U.S. government to respond positively to the initiatives of the USSR on [a] moratorium on nuclear testing, to review its decision to exceed SALT II ceilings, and to reconsider its Strategic Defense Initiative." It made no such appeal to the Soviet Union, which has a substantial head start in space weapons.[24] In its admonitions to both sides, the WCC endorsed the public propaganda line of the Soviet Union, and at the same time it criticized U.S. efforts to maintain an effective deterrent and to establish a non-nuclear defense shield against Soviet missiles.

Commenting on the 1983 Vancouver Assembly, the WCC's official journal *One World* (March 1987) underscored the oft-stated insistence on the tie between peace and justice: "The Sixth Assembly made it clear that WCC support for church-related and Christian groups in the North advocating nuclear disarmament must not divert attention from international ecumenical concern about oppressive structures affecting hundreds of millions in the South."[25]

CHAPTER THREE

Central America

IN JULY 1979 Christian leaders in Nicaragua played an important part in toppling the corrupt regime of President Anastasio Somoza de Bayle. Many of the "revolutionary Christians" who joined the alliance led by the Sandinista National Liberation Front (FSLN) viewed the merger of religion and Marxism as "a sign of hope for all of Latin America."[1] Subsequently, several Roman Catholic priests joined the Sandinista government, a pro-Cuban regime that embraced Marxist ideas and Leninist tactics.

This church activism, far from being a radical departure, fit neatly into the concept of "liberation theology" that flowered in Central America in the early 1970s. Liberation theology invokes such biblical concepts as the "kingdom of God," "justice," and "salvation" to justify Marxist revolutionary aims and methods, including violence.

Most liberation theologians regard the poor much as Marx regarded the proletariat—as the source of revolutionary liberation from feudalism and other traditional social and political structures. Other Marxist concepts frequently appear in liberationist writings as well; for example, revolution is deemed a "just war" against "structural violence." Religion and revolution become intertwined to such a degree that Christian participation in revolutions is deemed all but obligatory.[2]

This marriage of religion and revolutionary politics found widespread sympathy within the World Council of Churches. For years the WCC flirted with similar theological concepts about revolutionary movements in Africa and elsewhere in Latin America. A WCC team visiting Nicaragua shortly after the revolution saw a visible manifestation of this marriage and said it was convinced "of the determination of the government to initiate immediate innovative programs of reconstruction."[3]

Though events—as well as the personal testimony of former revolutionary leaders such as Eden Pastora and Alfonso Robelo—showed that the Sandinistas' commitment to Marxism was incompatible with the stated democratic goals of the Nicaraguan revolution, the WCC's faith in the Nicaragua experiment was not shaken. On the contrary, the Council did not respond to the Nicaraguan Commission of Jurists' report that 8,655 persons had been killed in Sandinista prisons between 1979 and 1983. Moreover, Charles R. Harper of the WCC's Human Rights Resources Office on Latin America, said the Council would no longer support the Permanent Commission for Human Rights in Managua since human rights had been guaranteed by the Nicaraguan government.[4]

Though the press in Nicaragua was censored, prisoners tortured, Indian minorities forcibly relocated, and some churches burned, the WCC at its Vancouver Assembly in 1983 pronounced the Nicaraguan people as "life-affirming" and "commended the Nicaraguan Christian community for its active participation in the building of national institutions and reconciliatory processes leading to peace and justice."[5] This vague language could easily be construed as an indirect blessing of the Managua regime.

The "People's Church"

Despite the support many Christians had given the guerrillas in their struggle against Somoza, once in power the Sandinista government launched a campaign of harassment and worse against the churches in Nicaragua. It supported a "popular" or "people's" church to lure Catholics away from the traditional or "reactionary" church. This blatant threat to the Catholic Church's authority compelled Pope John Paul II, in August 1982, to accuse the so-called popular church of yielding to political ideologies and sowing discord. The WCC, nonetheless, continued to sympathize with the popular church.

Despite a spate of arrests of Catholic priests and Moravian Church ministers, a WCC team in 1981 could find "no recognizable 'persecution' of the Church" in Nicaragua. After all, the team's report contended, the "Institute of Nicaraguan Cinema, under the Ministry of Culture, has produced a film called *Gracias a Dios y la Revolución* ["Thanks to God and the Revolution"] about Christian participation in the revolution."[6]

Three years later, ten Catholic priests were expelled from Nicaragua for what the Sandinistas termed "anti-government activity." The expulsion followed a march by more than three hundred people (five of the ten expelled priests were among them) led by Archbishop Miguel Obando y Bravo of Managua, in support of Father Amada Pena, who was accused of aiding anti-Sandinista rebels. According to the archbishop, "This is evidence that Marxism is trying to eliminate the Church in Nicaragua because Marxism is the enemy of the Church."[7]

Amnesty International later investigated the incident and found that the Sandinistas had fabricated the evidence against Father Pena.[8] The WCC Central Committee, meeting in Geneva at the time, ignored Father Pena's arrest, and Emilio Castro of Uruguay, who became the new WCC general secretary in January 1985, said that "it is totally unfair to talk about clamping down on religious freedom in Nicaragua."[9]

Indian Minorities

In 1979, the Sandinistas began to integrate the indigenous people of the Atlantic coast into the "revolutionary process." Most of the Miskito Indians in the region were Moravian Christians who were living on their ancestral lands. Because they had been ill-treated by Somoza, many of the Miskitos had initially sympathized with the Sandinistas. But during their forced relocation and subsequent persecution, the Indians resisted, and the FSLN responded savagely. There is evidence that one-fourth of the 165,000 Indians either have been relocated or are in refugee camps; one-half of the Indians' villages have been destroyed; one thousand Indian civilians are in prison, missing, or dead; and the Indians' civil rights have been seriously violated.[10]

The Sandinistas insist that the relocation was necessary because of guerrilla activities in the area where the Indians lived, but the relocation began well before there was any anti-Sandinista resistance in the region.

When, at the Vancouver Assembly in 1983, the WCC finally took notice of the Sandinistas' war against the Indians, it accepted the Sandinistas' explanation of the incidents. The Council said that the Nicaraguan government "had demonstrated its openness in acknowledging the inappropriateness of some policies related to the Miskito Indian and other ethnic groups of the Atlantic Coast, and is moving towards reconciliation."[11] A "Progress Report" on the Miskito Indians, published by the WCC's Commission on Inter-Church Aid, Refugee, and World Service, suggested that the Indians should cooperate with the government as much as possible.[12]

This is a far cry from the stance toward the Indians in other lands. In June 1982, for example, the Central Committee adopted a statement on "Land Rights for Indigenous Peoples" that indicted Australia, Brazil, Canada, Chile, Colombia, Guatemala, Mexico, New Zealand, Paraguay, the Philippines, Puerto Rico, and the United States for mistreating ethnic minorities. There was no mention of Nicaragua.

The Vancouver Assembly's "Statement on Central America" said little about Nicaragua beyond affirming and encouraging "the process of reconciliation among Nicaraguan minorities and the Spanish-speaking majority" and urging "the Nicaraguan government to maintain its openness and commitment to increasing the sensitivity of its policy and practice in this area."[13]

Backing the Sandinistas

A WCC delegation visited Nicaragua in September 1983 and acknowledged that the policy of relocating the Indians had caused great resentment and that Indian leaders and pastors who protested the policy had been jailed for opposing the revolution. The delegation added, "The leadership of the Church supports the revolutionary process and insists that official actions taken against its institutions and employees are not a case of religious persecution."[14]

The WCC delegates further denied that the Sandinistas' goal was "to establish a totalitarian Marxist state," and were impressed by "the pluralism in the government, the service of Christians, lay and clergy, at every level of government." As for the press, "Though we are supporters of a free press, we can understand some of the particularities of Nicaragua that argue for the present press censorship." The Sandinistas' actions could be forgiven because their government was deemed "a sign and transmitter of hope."[15] With this evaluation, the WCC delegation recommended that the "churches world-wide . . . learn from the unique experiment being lived by the Nicaraguan sisters and brothers in the Christian communities."[16]

In July 1985, another WCC delegation visited Nicaragua, Honduras, Guatemala, and El Salvador. In Nicaragua, it contacted only government and pro-government groups. In reporting their travels to the subsequent Central Committee meeting in Buenos Aires, also in 1985, some members of the delegation admitted that they had paid little or no attention to groups inside Nicaragua that opposed the Sandinistas, as, for example, the Roman Catholic archdiocese led by Cardinal Miguel Obando y Bravo. The archbishop, a former critic of the Somoza dictatorship, had become a stern critic of the Sandinistas.[17]

While in Nicaragua, the delegation endorsed liberation theology, a position reflected in a "pastoral letter" adopted by the Central Committee in Buenos Aires. The letter expressed sympathy with the Sandinistas and noted that the United States was involved "in support for the present government in El Salvador; in promoting militarization of Costa Rica and Honduras; in economic and diplomatic measures as well as constantly increasing military threats against Nicaragua."[18] The East German Communist newspaper *Neues Deutschland* praised the WCC for "chastising U.S. policy in Central America."[19]

El Salvador

The 1982 elections, which drew 70 percent of El Salvador's electorate to the polls despite a leftist guerrilla campaign of harassment and intimidation, and the 1984 elections, which won the presidency for José Napoleón Duarte, seemed ample justification of U.S. policy. Soon after Duarte's victory, right-wing death squad killings dropped off sharply and civilian casualties in the civil war also diminished, if more slowly. U.S. aid to the former military regime in El Salvador had made elections feasible, and thus furthered the cause of parliamentary democracy there.

The WCC thought differently. At its 1983 Vancouver Assembly, the Council made a point not to include the Salvadoran 1982 elections in what it termed "promising signs of life" in Latin America. It also declined to note the failure of the anti-government guerrillas' call to Salvadorans for a "final offensive" in January 1981.

The Vancouver statement went on to urge "the government of El Salvador to enter into a fruitful process of dialogue with representatives of its political and military opposition,"[20] even after popular support for this opposition had dwindled significantly as democratic reforms took hold. The WCC claimed that "the Christian Democratic Party" led by Duarte "does not have the least amount of popular support."[21] The Vancouver Assembly criticized the Salvadoran government for having "demonstrated an inability to curb human rights violations and implement needed reform."[22] On balance, the Assembly saw only the negative aspects of U.S. involvement in Central America. That the United States pressed for reform and aided democratic development was completely ignored—not only by the Assembly, but by almost every WCC statement on Central America. Subsequently, after his election to the presidency of El Salvador in 1985, Duarte began a dialogue with guerrillas, only to have his daughter kidnapped. She was later returned. But the WCC has never commented on this act of terror.

Target: "American Imperialism"

From its inception, the democratic movement in El Salvador has prompted a series of WCC statements, letters, and documents that reveal a pronounced anti-American slant. They viewed the Sandinista revolution as a triumph over "American imperialism" and therefore as a model for all Latin American countries.

Given this stance, the WCC's response to a wave of violence by the right-wing death squads in El Salvador in the late 1970s and early 1980s was predictable, as was the lack of response to leftist revolutionary violence. The WCC World Conference on Mission and Evangelism in Melbourne in May 1980 issued a "Declaration on El Salvador" recommending that a letter be sent to the U.S. President asking the American government to "stop support and military aid to military regimes, and to respect the right of the people of Latin America to seek a new social order that is more just and more humane."[23]

There was more of the same in the next few years. In a 1981 letter to the Latin America Council of Churches, for example, WCC General Secretary Philip Potter charged that the American administration "claims an improvement in the human rights situation in order to continue military and economic assistance."[24] And at the Central Committee's meeting in Dresden, East Germany, later that year, Washington was once again asked "to desist from all direct or covert, present or planned intervention in the countries of Central America and the Caribbean."[25]

Occasionally there were hints that countries other than the United States were involved in Central American conflicts. At the Vancouver

Assembly, for instance, the Council opposed "any type of military intervention by the United States, covert or overt, or by any other government in the Central American region," but the WCC's double standard effectively prohibited it from naming Cuba and the Soviet Union as well as other Soviet bloc countries as Sandinista allies and active supporters of revolutionary violence in El Salvador and elsewhere in Latin America.

In spite of compelling evidence to the contrary, the WCC persists in downplaying Soviet influence. This may be because the Soviet Union's proxy, Cuba, is looked upon with favor by both the WCC and the Conference of Caribbean Churches. The Council's Commission of the Churches in International Affairs (CCIA), for example, urges that "normal diplomatic relations" and trade "between the United States and Cuba be re-established."[26] Cuba—its domestic repression and its foreign policies, including its extensive military operations in Africa— is all but immune from WCC criticism.

In its condemnation of "American imperialism" in Central America, the WCC never mentioned the great disparity of U.S. and Soviet military and economic aid to the region. Moscow subsidizes Castro's Cuba to the extent of $6 million a day. There is no comparable subsidy by Washington to any regime in the area. In 1983–85, Soviet bloc economic and military aid to Cuba and Nicaragua was $15.85 billion, while U.S. aid to all of Central America was $3.14 billion.[27] By the end of 1984, Moscow was providing ten times as much military assistance to Nicaragua and Cuba as Washington was to all of Latin America. From 1981 to 1986, Soviet military aid to the Sandinistas approximated $1 billion, including $600 million in 1986 alone. In 1987, Washington is providing $70 million in military aid to the democratic resistance in Nicaragua. By 1985, the Sandinista army of 75,000 was supported by more than 10,000 military "advisors" from Cuba, the USSR, East Germany, Libya, and the Palestine Liberation Organization. As of early 1987, there were fifty-five U.S. military advisors in El Salvador and about 1,000 troops in Honduras to support joint exercises. There were no other U.S. forces in Central America, except for 10,000 stationed in the Southern Command in Panama to safeguard the canal and other U.S. interests throughout Latin America, an area ten times larger than Western Europe, where there are 300,000 American troops.

These verifiable facts about comparative U.S. and Soviet military and political influence in Cuba and Nicaragua appeared to have little impact on WCC thinking. So did reports and books by former victims of Cuban oppression, such as *Against All Hope* by Armando Valladares, published in 1986,[28] which revealed Castro's abuse of prisoners and the persecution of Christians. WCC staff.members who visit Cuba are apt to return as enthusiastic about Cuban policy as they were before. Valladares, a Cuban Christian and poet released in 1982 after twenty-two years' imprisonment in Cuba, writes about what this has meant to those who suffer for their faith:

> During those years, with the purpose of forcing us to abandon our religious beliefs and to demoralize us, the Cuban Communist indoctrinators repeatedly used the statements of support for Castro's revolution made by some representatives of American Christian churches. Every time that a pamphlet was published in the United States, every time a clergyman would write an article in support of Fidel Castro's dictatorship, a translation would reach us, and that was worse for the Christian political prisoners than the beatings or the hunger. Incomprehensibly to us, while we waited for the embrace of solidarity from our brothers in Christ, those who were embraced were our tormentors.[29]

Yet a member of the WCC's Commission on the Churches' Participation in Development had earlier waxed lyrical in praise of Castro's Communist regime: "Our group is struggling to find some categories by which to judge the 'Cuban experience' and wondering how to communicate this back to our countries and our churches. I notice that all of us when talking seem to imply that Cuban society shows a lot more signs of the Kingdom of God than many other societies we know of."[30] Most competent observers would hold that Jeane Kirkpatrick's characterization in 1987 is nearer the mark: "Cuba has been wholly protected against the censure of U.N. bodies while driving more than a million of its citizens into exile and imprisoning countless others for purely political offenses. More than any other country in the Americas, Cuba has repressed freedom of speech, religion, assembly, [and] press and denied its citizens the right to emigrate."[31]

CHAPTER FOUR

Afghanistan

IN DECEMBER 1979, Soviet armed forces invaded neighboring Afghanistan, ostensibly at the request of Kabul's Marxist government, which had come to power with Soviet aid in a military coup earlier that year. The worldwide protests that ensued, including those voiced by the United States, heightened as the Afghan resistance fighters fought the Soviet Goliath and hundreds of thousands of Afghans fled to nearby Pakistan.

The World Council of Churches waited nearly two months before commenting on the Soviet attack. In February 1980, in a unanimous statement entitled "Threats to Peace," the WCC's Executive Committee referred to "the military action by the USSR in Afghanistan" as "the latest direct, armed intervention in one country by another" that had "heightened the tension."[1] This highly unusual criticism of Moscow was blunted after the WCC became involved in church-sponsored humanitarian work among Afghan refugees. The Council's position on the Soviet invasion and occupation was mild.

This tepidity contrasts with the WCC's emphatic response to earlier armed invasions. When, for example, North Korean troops invaded South Korea in 1950, the WCC's Central Committee immediately denounced the attack as "an act of aggression."[2] That was three decades before the WCC fell under the strong influence of Soviet and Third World member churches. It was only after the influential Russian Orthodox Church joined the WCC in 1961 that the Council began to change its views toward the policies of the Soviet Union, though this shift cannot be wholly attributed to pressure from Orthodox delegates.[3] The change was gradual, for when Soviet troops crushed the Czechoslovakian Prague Spring Movement in August 1968, the WCC immediately issued a statement decrying "this ill-considered action by the USSR and its allies."[4]

27

But by the time of the Soviet invasion of Afghanistan, the WCC had changed dramatically. Its response was so weak and belated that the protests against the invasion by some member churches put severe pressure on the Council. The dissenting WCC members proposed a stronger condemnation of the Soviet attack, but their efforts failed and a compromise was reached.

The Executive Committee's "Threats to Peace" compromise was adopted after a serious debate between two conflicting views within the WCC. One side insisted that the Soviet invasion was a grave threat to world peace. The other side linked the Afghanistan war with other international issues—especially the policies of the United States and NATO. This latter view was pressed by Archbishop Kirill of Leningrad, who represented the Russian Orthodox Church on the WCC Executive Committee. Kirill drew a direct line between the Soviet invasion and NATO's deployment of new missiles in Europe in the final weeks of 1979. He did not point out that the NATO missiles were intended to offset the Soviet SS-20 ballistic missiles already in place and to guard cities and military facilities from Oslo to Istanbul. Besides, Kirill argued, the Soviet government had only responded to a request by the Afghanistan government that feared outside aggression, presumably by U.S.-supported Pakistani forces.

The vague and ambiguous Executive Committee compromise blunted condemnation of the Soviet invasion by placing it in a larger context of "threats to peace" such as the increasing number of "armed interventions by foreign powers" (unspecified), "the decision of NATO countries to deploy more than 500 'theater nuclear weapons' in Europe," the "worsening of economic relations between developed and developing nations," and tendencies by "certain nations [unspecified] to be militarily the most powerful."[5]

This compromise did not wholly satisfy the Russian Orthodox Church, so on March 20, 1980, the Holy Synod of the Russian church gave its direct official endorsement of the invasion: "We, churchmen, understand and accept the reasons which prompted the Soviet government to take such a step."[6] Hopes for a future WCC condemnation of the Afghanistan invasion waned.

Melbourne, May 1980

The first major WCC meeting after the compromise statement on Afghanistan was held in Melbourne, Australia, in May 1980. Its theme,

"Your Kingdom Come," was fraught with political overtones. The Conference's slogan, "Stop Repression in El Salvador!," seemed to demand an official statement on Afghan repression, too, since the horror being visited upon the Afghan people by the Soviet invasion dwarfed whatever was going on in El Salvador. But the Russian Orthodox Church was able to thwart any such attempt with the aid of the Latin American delegates and, now predictably, the U.S. delegates. At their own initiative, delegations from several American churches invited the Soviet representatives to an unscheduled evening meeting to discuss the churches' role as "agents of reconciliation." At the meeting, the Americans and Russians agreed to exclude the Soviet invasion from Conference deliberations in favor of less divisive issues, such as the churches' role in proclaiming peace.[7]

But some spirited delegates would not allow the issue to die. As Dutch delegate Anton Voss told the Conference: "If Latin America is mentioned, why not name what is in the center of the world's attention at the moment, namely the invasion of Afghanistan? If we don't mention Afghanistan here, the WCC will be in danger of not being taken seriously."[8] Gunnar Stalsett of Norway joined in by stating that the Afghan people's right of self-determination had been violated and that the WCC could not hide the fact and remain credible. Some Third World delegates agreed, but the Russians stood firm. Finally, in another compromise document both vague and weak, no countries were identified specifically in the statement on "Human Struggles."

Still, the issue refused to die. There were several other attempts to introduce the Afghanistan affair into the proceedings. On the last day, for example, Michael Nazir-Ali of Pakistan proposed that the Conference condemn the Soviet military action and its repression of human rights in Afghanistan. Russian Orthodox Bishop Makary immediately spoke up, insisting that the "aim of this Conference is to unite us." Another Russian delegate asserted that the Russian church's "participation in the WCC would be subject to reconsideration" should the Conference condemn the Soviet invasion.[9]

After another deadlock, the Conference adopted a resolution admitting that the WCC had not officially addressed certain international issues. "We may be able to identify some of those countries and people," the resolution said. "Others, however, we dare not identify for the simple reason that [to do so] may endanger the position—even the lives—of many of our brothers and sisters. . . . We know that many of them suffer under different regimes for their faith in Jesus Christ and urge that freedom of conscience be respected as well as other human rights. At the same time, we want to assure our unnamed brothers and sisters in many unnamed countries that we have not forgotten them; we identify strongly in their suffering for the kingdom of God."[10]

Central Committee Compromises

The same debate occupied the WCC's Central Committee when it met in August 1980 in Geneva. The question was whether to endorse the February 1980 "Threats to Peace" statement by the Executive Committee that had mildly but only superficially condemned the Soviet intervention. Several delegates expressed their disapproval of the WCC's one-sided handling of human rights violations. Per Loenning of Norway said that the Council should express its "solidarity with the suffering people of Afghanistan as well as some words about Kampuchea," formerly Cambodia, where from one to three million people had been systematically exterminated by the Pol Pot regime in three years. Loenning noted that the WCC had criticized the Vietnam War—and most especially the U.S. involvement in it—during the 1960s and 1970s, and thought it should speak out as emphatically about the Soviet invasion of Afghanistan.[11]

During the ensuing debate, Russian Orthodox Archbishop Kirill said it had been difficult for him to agree to the "Threats to Peace" text and his position (presumably with Soviet authorities) had worsened. WCC General Secretary Philip Potter again pointed out that the Afghan situation had not been addressed in isolation, but in a larger international context. Potter rationalized the disparity in tone between the WCC's statement on Afghanistan and its denunciation of North Korea's invasion of South Korea in 1950 by introducing irrelevant information under the rubric of moral symmetry. Afghanistan was not a Christian nation, Potter reminded the members, and "what is happening in Afghanistan is related to many other events" such as "the decisions made by NATO last December, to what is going on in the Middle East, the whole business of China, and all the rest."[12] Consciously or not, Potter's explanation reflected the Soviet Union's position on Afghanistan. The Soviets considered the invasion necessary to contain "threats to peace" in the region, including alleged attempts by China to destabilize the pro-Soviet Afghanistan government. Several WCC leaders were active in the Soviet-sponsored Christian Peace Conference, which also concerned itself with the Afghanistan issue.[13] A few days after the August 1980 Central Committee meeting, the Conference was convened in Budapest by its president, Hungarian Bishop Karoly Toth. Ninan Koshy, an official of the WCC, attended the meeting, just as Toth regularly attended WCC Central Committee meetings.[14] The Budapest meeting also concluded that the invasion should be viewed in its international context, that is, to be justified.[15]

Vancouver, Summer 1983

At the Sixth Assembly in Vancouver in 1983, the Soviet invasion of Afghanistan loomed large. After extensive talks with representatives from both the East and the West, the WCC leaders agreed to draft a statement that essentially endorsed the U.N. secretary general's efforts to find means to end the conflict in Afghanistan.[16] Since the Soviet Union had already approved the U.N. endeavor, the Soviet bloc delegates had no difficulty accepting the draft text. Many Western delegates, for their part, were simply relieved that the issue was seeing the light of day. (The final text of the statement on Afghanistan is carried in Appendix A.)

The draft text stated that a peaceful resolution of the conflict depended upon several conditions: (1) The supply of arms to resistance fighters by outside governments and groups must stop; (2) Afghan refugees must be given permission to return to their homeland; (3) a peace settlement must be agreed to by the Soviet Union, the United States, the People's Republic of China, and Pakistan; and (4) Soviet troops would be withdrawn from Afghanistan in the context of a general political settlement, including an agreement between Afghanistan and the USSR.[17]

The Russian Orthodox delegates called the draft statement "balanced and realistic"; any other text, they added, would be unacceptable. Potter and the CCIA staff backed the Russians. And, since the four conditions had been lifted from the U.N. proposals, no serious opposition was expected at the Assembly's plenary session. But, contrary to expectations, the draft generated considerable opposition. Pakistan's Bishop Alexander Malik, for instance, proposed that the resolution be amended to call for "unconditional withdrawal of Soviet troops from Afghanistan." Malik further charged that the drafting committee had "selected the weakest possible language. If it had been any Western country, the WCC would have jumped on it and denounced the country in the strongest possible language."[18]

Malik's proposal was rejected, but the debate continued. Finally, Bishop David Preus of the American Lutheran Church proposed lifting the requirement that outside countries stop supplying arms to Afghan resistance fighters and recommended the "immediate" withdrawal of Soviet troops. The Russian Orthodox delegates spurned Preus's proposals—Metropolitan Yuvenali said that anything suggesting an unconditional withdrawal of Soviet troops from Afghanistan would be rejected.

The Russians were looking for a double guarantee: that outside groups stop supplying the Afghan resistance forces, and that the Soviet occupation be condoned until "an overall political settlement" could be reached between Moscow and its puppet regime. This would, in effect, authorize the invader to set the terms of withdrawal. As finally adopted, the WCC resolution would admit only that "the continuing fighting" in Afghanistan "has led to tremendous suffering for vast sections of the population, many of whom have become refugees." It neither condemned the Soviet Union for the invasion, nor identified the cause of the subsequent suffering. It added that the U.N. secretary general's proposed agreement would "contribute to improvement of relations between the USA and USSR and of international relations in general."[19] This is an expression of moral symmetry mitigated by vagueness.

CHAPTER FIVE

Southern Africa

SOUTHERN AFRICA WITH its nine states in widely different stages of political, economic, and cultural development is a complex, turbulent, and strategically important region. The Republic of South Africa is in many respects a modern industrial state—a First World country, though a majority of its black population lives in "Third World" conditions. It has vast reserves of gold and strategic materials and commands the vital sea route around the cape. The neighboring Frontline States, Angola, Zambia, Zimbabwe, and Mozambique, are politically unstable and are for the most part ruled by black, one-party dictatorships. Angola and Mozambique are former Portuguese colonies, and each is challenged by "freedom fighters" who seek to overthrow the existing regime. These resistance movements have received modest support from South Africa and the United States from time to time. For decades the Soviet Union has sought to gain a foothold in this strategic region, with the ultimate objective of establishing a pro-Soviet regime in South Africa. In Angola, as of early 1987, the minority regime in Luanda was propped up by some 37,000 Cuban, 2,500 Soviet, and 2,500 East German military personnel.

Since 1975, the World Council of Churches has selectively and sporadically addressed a few of the problems in southern Africa, but through a lens that focuses almost exclusively on "white racism," capitalism, and Western imperialism as the fundamental problems and revolutionary movements and socialism as the answer. This approach has expressed itself in both words and deeds, the latter through large grants of money to Marxist-supported revolutionary movements like SWAPO (South West Africa People's Organization) and the ANC (African National Congress). In the name of racial justice, SWAPO seeks power by force in Namibia and the ANC is seeking to overthrow by violence the white regime in Pretoria. SWAPO cadres have been

33

trained in the Soviet Union, Cuba, and other Soviet bloc countries. We will first examine the WCC's deeds and rationale, and then review its pronouncements on South Africa.

Support for "Liberation Movements"

One of the more praiseworthy aims of the WCC has been expressed in its "Program to Combat Racism," established in 1969. The program's objectives include financial aid to "organizations of oppressed racial groups or organizations supporting victims of racial injustice whose purposes are not inconsonant with the general purposes of the World Council."[1] This crusade, however, soon lost sight of its objectives and veered off into supporting revolutionary political causes.[2] By January 1987, the program's Special Fund to Combat Racism had expended $6,906,545 for such causes.[3]

The Council's World Consultation on "Racism in the 1980s," held in Noordwijkerhout, Holland, in 1983, denounced "naive assumptions such as the one that racism is a phenomenon which can be isolated from capitalism and imperialism." Not only has "the international capitalist economic system" provided the foundation of "much of the racism experienced by people in the world today," but it is also the "one ordered to promote the self-interest, greed, and values of the 'white' world."[4]

The WCC's Central Committee hailed these reports and commended them to member churches. Its stamp of approval narrowed the scope of the war on racism to such an extent that the Council has found it awkward to address racial injustices not directly attributed to capitalism—such as the treatment of Soviet Jews or the Sandinistas' abuses of the Miskito Indians in Nicaragua. The 1979 Central Committee meeting in Jamaica, for example, considered the "racism of white people" as "the most dangerous and powerful phenomenon that needed to be combatted more urgently than any other form of racism or ethnocentrism. By implication, concentration on South Africa became mandatory."[5] The WCC's doctrine for combatting racism was translated into support for revolutionary violence.

In 1983, the WCC's Special Fund to Combat Racism gave $70,000 to the ANC and $105,000 to SWAPO. Both groups espouse violent revolution, and both groups are supported politically and militarily by the Soviet Union. Paul Raveloson, secretary of the ANC's external coordinating committee, told the English-language *Japan Times* in early June 1987 that "the ANC is receiving arms and weapons directly from the Soviet Union and some ANC officers went to the Soviet Union for military training."[6] These organizations have continued to receive WCC support, including $80,000 to the ANC and $110,000 to SWAPO in 1986, despite their persistent use of terrorism. Controversy has attended every Council grant to the ANC, SWAPO, and similar groups, but the more recent complaints have been mild compared to the uproar generated in August 1978 when the WCC made an admittedly "political" decision to give $85,000 to the "Patriotic Front" that was seeking violently to overthrow the biracial regime of Rhodesia, since renamed Zimbabwe. Though the Council has professed a desire not to identify with any particular political party, Front leaders Robert Mugabe and Joshua Nkomo described the grant as an "endorsement by the WCC of its armed struggle."[7] The WCC justified the favoritism by suggesting that the Patriotic Front was more committed to eliminating racism than the other black liberation groups in the region. (A month later, the WCC gave $125,000 to SWAPO.)

The Zimbabwe grant was especially controversial for reasons beyond the Patriotic Front's ties to Cuba and the Soviet Union and the avowed Marxism of one of its leaders. The Front had also deliberately murdered innocent missionaries—such as seven Roman Catholics slain in February 1977—and other Christians, as, for instance, the June 1978 attack on a Pentecostal missionary post during which three men, five women, and four children were killed.[8]

The Council's response was to exonerate the Patriotic Front. "The atrocities perpetuated by all sides," the WCC stated, "are clearly the result of the regime's persistent refusal to negotiate a peaceful settlement with the Zimbabwe leaders."[9]

WCC sympathies were even more blatantly displayed in 1978 when the guerrillas shot down a civilian Air Rhodesia plane, an act that resulted in the death of thirty-eight of the fifty-six passengers. According to a *Newsweek* account, a group of survivors, confronted by a band of black guerrillas, pleaded for mercy. "The blacks opened fire with their Soviet-made Kalashnikov rifles. The next day, when Rhodesian paratroops dropped into the area, they found ten bodies, including those of seven women and two young girls, scattered across the bloodsodden field."[10]

The Council, though "deeply" deploring the "reported shooting down" of the civilian aircraft, nevertheless declined to identify the culprits, though Nkomo had already personally claimed credit for the atrocity.[11]

Criticism of WCC Grants

The WCC's biased approach to the Rhodesian problem provoked severe criticism from member churches in Norway, Switzerland, West Germany, and elsewhere. Both the Salvation Army and the Presbyterian Church of Ireland first suspended their membership and later withdrew entirely. The Irish church leaders argued that grants to groups such as the Patriotic Front would be interpreted as a WCC endorsement of terrorist violence, something with which the Irish were all too familiar.

The controversy came to a head at the WCC Central Committee meeting in Jamaica in January 1979. There, the Salvation Army's Harry Williams, supported by David Russell of the Baptist Union of Great Britain and Ireland, proposed that, when the WCC's Special Fund to Combat Racism awarded grants, "use should be made wherever possible of indigenous church agencies to deliver the humanitarian services desired."[12] Their intent was to prevent WCC bodies, such as the Executive Committee, from making grants to groups solely on the basis of politics.

WCC General Secretary Philip Potter would have none of it. The Russell-Williams proposal would, he said, "strike at a basic purpose of the grants from the Special Fund, namely, to express the WCC's solidarity with those struggling for freedom and justice."[13] Potter persuaded Williams and Russell to withdraw the proposal by repeating a promise that the Special Fund would consult with WCC member churches in the matter of grants. In the end, the Central Committee had the last word. It announced that administration of the Special Fund "has so far been in accordance with the established and accepted criteria set by the Central Committee," and encouraged the Program to Combat Racism to conduct its business as usual.[14]

Potter's attempt to paper over differences was short-lived. The 1983 Consultation on "Racism in the 1980s" was so blatantly anti-Western that the rift in the Council over its revolutionary politics deepened. Two years before, the Salvation Army—the world's largest non-governmental social welfare organization and a founding member of the WCC—had withdrawn its full membership, retaining only fraternal status. Salvation Army spokesmen said the decision was based on opposition to WCC policies and actions that "we regard as political, and which, as such, endanger the non-political nature of the Army."[15] The Central Committee received the news "with deep regret," but disagreed with the distinction drawn by the Salvation Army "between the so-called political nature of the action of the WCC and the claim of the Salvation Army to have a non-political stance."[16]

Tribal Violence in Zimbabwe

The favor granted the Patriotic Front in Zimbabwe by the WCC was again very much in evidence in 1979 when all parties of that war-torn country agreed to engage in constitutional discussions in London. Though the British paid for the entire proceedings, the WCC gave the Patriotic Front delegation a special grant.

The WCC did not waver in its support even when Front leaders Mugabe and Nkomo refused to agree to a ceasefire and demanded that their forces be fully integrated into any future Zimbabwean army. So consistent was the Council's support for the Front that when Mugabe was elected Zimbabwe's prime minister, he thanked the Council for its "commitment to the principles for which you and we have struggled together."[17]

Many Council leaders viewed Mugabe's electoral victory in 1980 as a vindication of their policy and would brook no further criticism of Zimbabwe. Philip Potter, for example, vowed at the 1980 Central Committee meeting that the Council would "not be bullied by those who attack us for giving our attention to controversial political issues."[18]

The rude awakening came only a few months after Mugabe was in power. Supporters of the former allies Nkomo and Mugabe began to clash, bringing the country to the brink of civil war. Relations between the two deteriorated rapidly until in January 1982 Nkomo was accused of conspiring against Mugabe. Nkomo was dismissed as a government minister, imprisoned, and forced into temporary exile. Mugabe was finally presiding over what was for all practical purposes a one-party system. Further, he and his more numerous Shona tribe had prevailed over Nkomo and his smaller Matabele tribe. Such are the racist politics of Zimbabwe and many other black African states.

The first reports of the mass killings in Matabeleland by Mugabe's

North Korean–trained "Fifth Brigade" army units reached the West in February 1983. The brutality was accompanied by a crackdown on dissent within Zimbabwe, including new laws curbing the press.

Mugabe, who had once praised the Council's support for his struggle, now responded to cautious criticism with the demand that church leaders "leave the government and policies well alone and stick strictly to worship."[19]

There was a flicker of hope when Mugabe seemed to agree to a call by Roman Catholic bishops and the Anglican bishop of Matabeleland for investigations into the alleged atrocities. A WCC team that visited Zimbabwe "expressed confidence that the investigation would be thorough."[20] But one year later, the Catholic bishops again voiced their concern over the murder, rape, and torture of thousands of Matabele tribesmen.[21]

The turbulence also touched Mugabe's rivals. The former prime minister, Methodist Bishop Abel Muzorewa, was arrested on November 1, 1983, on charges of complicity with Israel and South Africa.[22] The WCC reacted slowly, when at all, in an admittedly confused situation. The Council issued no statement on behalf of Bishop Muzorewa or any other political prisoners. As for the killings in Matabeleland, a WCC spokesman said in 1984 that, though the matter was of "very serious concern for the WCC," not all situations are dealt with by making public statements and "we make no attempt to balance such statements."[23] (Zambia, Zimbabwe, and other Frontline regimes have harbored SWAPO and ANC terrorists for years, but in May 1987 the U.S. Senate voted 77–15 to deny economic aid to black-ruled states that support guerrilla attacks against South Africa.[24])

The WCC's preoccupation with "white racism" prevented it from dealing honestly with the "black racism" that expressed itself in discrimination or persecution by members of one African tribe against members of another tribe, or by discrimination or violence by blacks against white politicians or farmers. The Council showed little concern over the human rights violations by the many one-party black dictatorships in Africa.

Of even greater consequence, the WCC never addressed the human rights implications of the growing Soviet political and military influence in Zimbabwe. For years, Moscow by propaganda, political support, and direct military aid had been attempting to transform Zimbabwe into a client state and to establish there a military presence directed against South Africa. In April 1987, the *Sunday Telegraph* of London

SOUTHERN AFRICA   39

reported that Zimbabwe had purchased twelve MIG-29s—ten combat
aircraft and two trainers—for delivery in 1988.[25] The MIG-29 is the
Soviet Union's most advanced jet fighter. The planes would be accompanied by 180 Soviet pilots and other "technical advisors." Zimbabwe's defense minister said "no such purchases had been made,"
but acknowledged in Moscow on April 30, 1987, that he was shopping
around and thanked the Soviet Union for its support. According to
U.S. and British spokesmen, such a transaction would have serious
political and military implications for all of southern Africa and beyond.

South Africa

The WCC's grants to revolutionary groups are wholly consistent
with its formal pronouncements. At its Central Committee meeting in
Jamaica in January 1979, the Committee not only defended its substantial financial contributions to SWAPO and the ANC, but urged the
churches to support these and other Soviet-backed "liberation" movements seeking to overthrow the white government of South Africa.
The Committee's statement was a mixture of vague generalizations
and specific assertions (some of them true) that provided neither a
balanced nor an accurate picture of the problems facing that troubled
country and its varied population groups. There was no mention of the
Indians or coloreds, who at that time were denied—like the blacks—a
national political voice.

"The systematic repression of the black people has continued unabated," said the Committee, and "several black organizations and
black leaders and others fighting apartheid" have been banned.[26] No
reference was made to the numerous anti-apartheid newspapers, journals, churches, and other organizations that were permitted to operate
freely, or to the fact that virtually all the banned individuals or groups
either used or advocated the use of violence. The statement asserted
that "arrests, detentions, torture and deaths in detention have continued," but provided no evidence or documentation. It accused the
government of deliberately breaking up black families and condemned
the "sinister policy of carving out 'Bantustans.' " It lamented increased Western investment in South Africa and called for "disinvestment and cessation of bank loans."

The Committee condemned Pretoria-conducted elections in Namibia "in open defiance of the United Nations," whose General Assembly has recognized SWAPO as the sole legitimate representative of that trust territory.

There was no recognition of the history or complexity of the multi-racial and tribal situation in either South Africa or Namibia or of the fact that blacks enjoyed far greater economic and educational oppor-tunities—and greater protection under the law—in both countries than in most of the black-ruled states whose political elites do not permit elections or tolerate an independent judiciary.

Meeting in Dresden in August 1981, the Central Committee reaf-firmed its "rejection of apartheid" and focused on the South African government's efforts to relocate blacks from the illegal "squatter settlements" in Cape Province and send them to their "homelands."[27] It called upon all Christians to condemn "the South African regime's barbarous act of destroying African families" and to intensify their support of "all those, inside and outside the country, who are strug-gling for a just South Africa."

At the same meeting, the WCC's general secretary was authorized to cable U.N. General Secretary Waldheim expressing "concern about the attack of South African forces on Angola" and urging their imme-diate withdrawal. The Council expressed no concern over the fact that Moscow's client regime in Luanda was propped up by 25,000 or more Cuban troops and 5,000 Soviet and East German military personnel. Nor did it mention that South African assistance went to the pro-democratic UNITA (National Union for the Total Independence of Angola) guerrillas led by Jonas Savimbi.

The Vancouver Assembly in 1983, reaffirming past Central Commit-tee views, asserted: "Institutionalized racism in South Africa contin-ues to be the central problem of justice and peace in the region" because "white minority rule" causes "enormous suffering."[28] The Assembly condemned the "Bantustan policy," but in a rare statement acknowledged that "Bantustan [i.e., black] rule in many instances" was as "oppressive and arbitrary as . . . white rule" and "resulted in the proscription of churches and the systematic persecution of peo-ple." The statement said that the proposal to include Asians and coloreds in a "multicameral South African legislature" did "not in-volve any sharing of political power."

The Assembly condemned the "relentless refusal" of the South African government "to recognize SWAPO as the legitimate represen-tative of the Namibian people" and asserted that Pretoria's "insistence on linking the withdrawal of Cuban troops from Angola to Namibian independence is 'an irrelevance.' "

Turning to the region as a whole, the Vancouver delegates said: "During the last decade South Africa, with the active collaboration of major Western powers and Israel, has been engaged in a massive military build-up which now includes nuclear weapons capability" that "poses a major threat" to peace and stability. The statement condemned President Reagan's policy of "constructive engagement" and a $1.25 billion International Monetary Fund loan to a regime "pursuing a concerted policy of an 'undeclared war against its neighbors' through destabilization and aggression."

Ambiguity on the Use of Violence

The Vancouver statement reaffirmed the WCC's "abhorrence of all forms of violence" and at the same time urged support for organizations that advocate and use violence, "including the liberation movements recognized by the UN—which oppose apartheid and racism."[29] The Assembly called for "mandatory and comprehensive sanctions" against South Africa and urged "member churches to discourage their people from emigrating to South Africa."

The Central Committee meeting in Geneva in 1984 endorsed the Vancouver position and focused its attention on Namibia. In a rare and highly selective historical statement, the Committee recalled the German occupation of South West Africa (1884-1915) during which "more than 100,000 Namibians were slaughtered."[30] It described Namibia today as "a military camp" and urged the churches to "condemn South Africa's intensified campaign of deception through diplomacy" and to support U.N. resolutions "calling for mandatory sanctions." The statement condemned the state of emergency declared by the South African government and urged the release of "all political prisoners," which under the circumstances would have included those like Nelson Mandela, the ANC leader who was convicted for acts of criminal violence. It commended the "U.S., Scandinavia, and the Netherlands" for initiating sanctions against Pretoria.

In 1985, meeting in Buenos Aires, the Central Committee continued on the same line. One informed delegate pointed out that no South African church declared itself in support of disinvestment, but the Committee followed the advice of Bishop Desmond Tutu's South

African Council of Churches in calling for sanctions.[31] It made no mention of the fact that major black leaders, such as Chief Gatsha Buthelezi, who represents some six million Zulus, and Lucy Mvubelo, general secretary of the National Union of Clothing Workers, an influential black trade union in South Africa, have repeatedly and publicly rejected Bishop Tutu's position.[32] Alan Paton, author of *Cry the Beloved Country,* criticized Tutu for advocating disinvestment: "I do not understand how your Christian conscience allows you to advocate disinvestment. It would go against my deepest principles to advocate anything that would put a man—and especially a black man—out of a job." Paton continued, "Your morality is confused just as was the morality of the church in the Inquisition, or the morality of Dr. Verwoerd in his utopian dreams. You come near to saying that the end justifies the means, which is a thing no Christian can do."[33] To his credit, Bishop Tutu has on several occasions condemned black violence against alleged collaborators with the white regime.

In January 1987, the Central Committee meeting in Geneva issued a major pronouncement on southern Africa. Its picture of the troubled and tragic situation in South Africa ignored many relevant facts and distorted others. The Committee declared that the "black townships" were "totally militarized," that in Namibia "cruel and inhuman treatment of the populace remains the rule of the day," that South Africa's "destabilization of the Frontline States and the neighboring countries continues unabated," and that Pretoria's policies have "caused an astronomical $10 billion damage to their economies."[34] These statements are not sustained by facts.

No mention was made of the necklacing (burning people alive by igniting a tire filled with gasoline hung around their necks) of black moderates by black militants and other forms of black-against-black violence and terror, nor was there mention of the pupil boycott of township schools organized by militant leaders that deprived children of a year of education. As the result of joint efforts by the government, American business leaders, and others, the boycott was brought to a virtual end by early 1987 and greater resources were allocated the black schools.

The January 1987 Central Committee statement made no mention of any positive developments in South Africa. In fact, there have been many such developments. As one who has been visiting that troubled country since 1962, I saw for myself during a fact-finding visit in early 1987 significant evidence of constructive change. Many informed black, Indian, and white leaders of varying political views asserted that there was more progress in race relations and in broadening political participation in the past five years than in the previous fifty. The WCC's picture of the townships was closer to the distorted images portrayed on America's TV screens than to the flesh-and-blood realities on the ground. Turbulence in the townships is a reality, but it is an exception. Members of our fact-finding group walked freely about in Soweto and other black townships. There we visited nurseries for the children of working mothers that provided two meals a day, well-run schools, clinics, swimming pools, and other recreational facilities. We spoke with pastors of various denominations in their homes. Under the emergency measures undertaken largely to protect black lives and preserve a measure of order essential to continued movement toward greater justice, the police stations in the townships had been reinforced. After TV cameras were barred from the townships, there was a sharp decline in black violence, which suggests that some of the violence had been mounted by radical elements seeking to garner a worldwide audience for their cause.

The WCC also overlooked the extensive assistance that South Africa provides not only to the Frontline States but to many countries throughout black Africa in the key areas of transportation, technology, electric power, health, nutrition, and education. Nor was there any recognition that virtually all groups of all races (except for revolutionary organizations, the extreme left, and adherents of liberation theology) oppose economic and diplomatic sanctions. As far as I could ascertain, no church in South Africa unequivocally supported economic sanctions; on the contrary such punitive measures were widely considered both inhumane and counterproductive.

In January 1987, the Southern African Catholic Bishops' Conference issued a fourteen-page analysis prepared by its Special Commission on Economic Pressures. The commission expressed serious misgivings about the bishops' earlier endorsement of economic sanctions. Noting that eighty-six U.S. corporations had pulled out of South Africa and twenty-six more were "on the verge" of doing so, the commission said this action would lessen the constructive influence of American firms in improving black working conditions and increasing educational opportunities. It would also hurt the already depressed economy. Apart from throwing thousands of blacks out of work, the sanctions had virtually put a stop to substantial reforms by the government and encouraged the imposition of emergency measures. Since it is the

Church's mission to promote peaceful change, the commission found sanctions to be profoundly counterproductive.

The WCC took quite a different stance. According to its 1987 statement, its ultimate aim is to establish a "united, free and democratic South Africa." To this end the Council urged that letters of protest be sent to President P. W. Botha, that the disinvestment campaign be accelerated, that the churches step up their pressure on banks to "stop any new loans, credit or any other form of assistance," and that the rescheduling of the South African debt be made "dependent on the resignation of the Botha government."

Revolutionary violence was unambiguously justified by the WCC's Program to Combat Racism conference in Lusaka, Zambia, May 4 to May 8, 1987.[35] This conclusion was reached after intense discussions with ANC President Oliver Tambo and other ANC and SWAPO leaders on the essential role of violence in overthrowing the South African government. A few days before the Botha regime had received a mandate in the whites-only election to continue its substantial, gradual, constitutional, and nonviolent efforts to abolish apartheid and broad political participation.

Several delegates were impressed by Tambo's response to "an angry young man" who justified the "necklace" killing of suspected supporters of the Pretoria government. "Our struggle is not against people," Tambo responded, adding that parents, youths, and churches can together immobilize collaborators. Anglican Bishop John Boswell of Ontario said he was "deeply moved" by Tambo's views and would return to Canada declaring that "no Christian has the right to condemn these people for the use of force."

Bishop Boswell's support of Tambo was endorsed by the South Africa Council of Churches leader, the Rev. C. F. Beyers Naudé; the executive secretary of the Program to Combat Racism, Jean Sindab; the U.S. National Council of Churches' Africa director, Willis Logan; and the majority of other delegates in Lusaka. Interestingly enough, WCC General Secretary Emilio Castro, a self-declared pacifist, indirectly supported violence: "I do not have the right to impose [my pacifism] on my friends who see their children massacred every day."

The Lusaka WCC conference "justified" revolutionary violence against South Africa, but did not explicitly endorse the ANC and SWAPO, which advocate and use such violence, though it came close to doing so. The specific recommendations urged: (1) increased aid to liberation movements, (2) recognition of SWAPO as "the sole and authentic representative of the people of Namibia,'' (3) Washington's abandonment of its demand that Cuban troops withdraw from Angola before Namibia becomes independent, and (4) more pressure on Western governments and businesses to sever economic links with South Africa and Namibia.

In a telling statement, the WCC's Sindab commended the human contact between ANC, SWAPO, and Pan Africanist Congress leaders and the delegates that brought ''the churches' relations with the liberation movements out of the closet.'' He noted that the WCC had given small grants to all three of these groups for the past fifteen years, but that the Lusaka conference provided the first ''in-depth church–liberation movement dialogue'' on strategies for ending apartheid. The actual contributions to the three revolutionary groups from 1970 through 1986 totaled $2,494,500. In sum, the WCC's Program to Combat Racism and the WCC as a whole had lost confidence in peaceful and constitutional change and now favored revolutionary violence supported politically and militarily and to a significant extent led by the Soviet Union.

CHAPTER SIX

East Asia and
the Pacific

THE WESTERN PACIFIC basin now rivals the North Atlantic in industrial and commercial vigor. This was made possible by the post–World War II stability underwritten by the U.S. military presence in Japan, the Republic of Korea, and the Philippines, and American military aid to other friends and allies. This peace and prosperity are threatened by the growing Soviet military activity—air, naval, and submarine—in the area. North Korea, Vietnam, and other Communist states in the region have totalitarian regimes whose poverty and disregard for human rights contrast sharply with conditions in neighboring non-Communist countries. The principal threat to peace comes from the Soviet Union, North Korea, and Vietnam, and to a lesser extent from the People's Republic of China.[1]

The 1983 Vancouver Assembly of the World Council of Churches took notice of developments in the vast Pacific area, but made only two brief statements.[2] One focused exclusively on the South Pacific, urging that it become a nuclear-free zone and condemning past U.S. and recent French nuclear tests. The other statement criticized U.S. bases in the Philippines as "threats to the sovereignty, security and human rights of the Filipino people," and called for the bases to be closed. It made no mention of the massive Soviet military presence— air, naval, and submarine bases—in Vietnam, or of the Soviets' growing military presence throughout the Pacific. Neither did Vancouver delegates condemn human rights abuses in North Korea, Vietnam, or Cambodia. Indeed, the Assembly's one-sided condemnation of the West, in pronouncements that ignored the Soviet Union, China, and other Communist states, was characteristic of the WCC's stance on Pacific issues since the Council's 1975 Nairobi Assembly.

46

People's Republic of China

The WCC has seldom disapproved of the policies of Communist China. It was among the first organizations to insist on admitting the People's Republic of China (PRC) to the United Nations—concurrent with expulsion of the Republic of China on Taiwan. The WCC did express concern about brutal repression within the PRC during the Cultural Revolution of the 1960s—but only after the fact. Even so, many elements within the WCC continued to sympathize with the "Chinese experiment," which they described as creating a model society. Among the ecumenical elite, there were even those who compared Maoism with the Kingdom of God.[3]

When in 1978 the WCC received an urgent report from Amnesty International on "Political Imprisonment in the People's Republic of China," the Council refused to respond for fear it would be an affront to the churches and Christians in China.

Nor did the WCC react when, in the late 1970s, the Peking regime suppressed a dissident movement. One of the dissidents, Wei Jing-sheng, who edited the independent journal *Tansuo,* wrote a detailed description of the Chinese prison system and its methods of torture. Wei was arrested on March 29, 1979, and parts of his sensational trial were shown on Chinese television.[4] But no criticism came from the WCC.

The fate of dissidents in non-Communist Asian countries presented a quite different story. The Council was vocal about restrictions of religious freedom in the Republic of China on Taiwan. The WCC has particularly close ties to the Presbyterian Church of Taiwan (PCT), which had serious clashes with the Taipei government. In 1970, for example, PCT leaders called for the admission of mainland China into the United Nations.

Presbyterian leaders also participated in mass demonstrations in Taiwan on "Human Rights Day" in December 1979. Among those arrested was the PCT general secretary, the Rev. Mr. Kao. The WCC did respond to this arrest. In April 1980, WCC General Secretary Philip Potter sent a telegram to President Chiang Ching-kuo of Taiwan, expressing the Council's "great shock and concern" over Mr. Kao's arrest and demanding "his immediate release."[5] Within days, dele-gates from the WCC and the World Alliance of Reformed Churches traveled to Taiwan to protest Kao's arrest and demonstrate their solidarity with the PCT. They expressed regret that when the Taiwanese Prebyterians "began to articulate the relevance of the Christian Gospel to their daily life," they " became the object of persecution. Freedom of religion means more than simply the freedom of worship; it means freedom to live out the implications of one's faith as well."[6] The principle was right, but it was selectively applied.

Korea and the Philippines

Korea is another chapter in the same story. The Republic of Korea in the South—not the Communist government of North Korea— has received the brunt of WCC criticism. In 1979, for example, a Council CCIA report denounced South Korea for its human rights policies, but had little to say about North Korea, though independent sources such as Freedom House had judged North Korea far more harshly than the South Korean government for rights abuses. North Korea is a brutal totalitarian state seeking to subvert an authoritarian government in South Korea that respects many rights denied in the North. CCIA Director Leopoldo Niilus, apparently in an attempt to forestall criticism of his organization, wrote: "The publication of this report is not without risks. Similar publications have in the past been used as propaganda tools of North Korea, with the consequent labelling by South Korean authorities of its authors as Communist agitators."[7]

If North Korea were once again to attack the South, one wonders whether the WCC would censure it as it did in 1950. Since 1960, the WCC has added a large number of Soviet bloc churches, most if not all of whose delegates support North Korea.

The WCC has also kept a sharp eye out for infringements of human rights in the Philippines. In September 1977, Potter sent a cable to President Ferdinand Marcos asking him "to grant general and unconditional amnesty to all political prisoners and to restore the human rights and fundamental freedoms of the people."[8] Potter also protested the "suppression of people's movements struggling for social and economic justice" and called attention to the detention of Senator Jovito Salongo, a member of the WCC's Commission on International Affairs, and to the activities of leaders of the Christian Movement, a left-wing organization.[9]

These WCC actions were arguably legitimate—there certainly were human rights violations under the Marcos government. But at times a revealing political element crept into Council directives. For example, the Council often criticized the U.S. military presence in the Philippines. According to Leopoldo Niilus, "the perspective of the victims of militarization" is different from that of those who make U.S. policy. Niilus further charged that there is a "direct correlation between militarization and human rights."[10]

The 1983 Vancouver Assembly took it from there. It spoke of "the negative effects of the continuation of U.S. military bases in the Philippines" and said that the "presence of these foreign conventional and nuclear forces poses a threat to the sovereignty, security, and human rights of the Filipino people." The Assembly asked the Council's general secretary "to recommend to the churches appropriate actions in support of the churches in the Philippines and the efforts of the Filipino people for the withdrawal of the bases."[11]

Apparently obsessed by the presence of the U.S. military facilities (actually the bases are owned by the Manila government, which leases them to the Americans) in the Philippines, the WCC was unable to recognize that U.S. administrations repeatedly pressed Marcos for human rights reforms. Indeed, without substantial American pressure, President Marcos would not have fled in February 1986, clearing the way for Corazon Aquino to assume the presidency.

Vietnam

In 1973, two years before Saigon fell to the North Vietnamese army, the WCC's Commission on World Mission and Evangelism asked the North Vietnamese government in Hanoi to receive an international delegation to express their solidarity with those who had been "terrorized" by the American bombing. This request was typical of the WCC's stance on the Vietnam War. The Council consistently refused to acknowledge that North Vietnam had a hand in the devastation of Indochina, but it censured the U.S. presence "in any form" in Vietnam as "detrimental to the peace in Indochina."[12] The Council also condemned U.S. and South Vietnamese military operations in Laos and Cambodia, but ignored or played down North Vietnamese activities in these same countries.

A few months after the conclusion of the 1973 Paris Agreement to end the war between North and South Vietnam, the WCC demanded that the government in South Vietnam "release all political prisoners" and "immediately restore the democratic liberties for which the Agreement provides." But it made no mention of political detainees in North Vietnam.[13]

Unlike Council leaders' condemnation of the North Korean aggression against South Korea in 1950, there was little WCC response to the massive North Vietnamese invasion of South Vietnam in March 1975. The Council's Executive Committee, meeting in Geneva, produced a mild statement appealing "to the signatories" of the Paris Agreement "to comply with its provisions" and "urged all states outside Vietnam to refrain from any military involvement or presence in South Vietnam." The meaning was clear. In the opinion of the Executive Committee, the United States was the oppressor if not the aggressor in Vietnam, not the North Vietnamese Communists who had invaded South Vietnam and had violated the territorial integrity of Cambodia.

The statement barely touched on the tragedy of the hundreds of thousands of people fleeing their homes in South Vietnam, and noted only "that the majority of people have remained in their places as control of territory has changed."[14] Later that year, when Cambodia and Laos fell to Marxist forces, the WCC continued to view the fateful events as purely internal affairs.

After the fall of Saigon in 1975, the Communist regime in Hanoi imposed its will over the entire country and the situation deteriorated rapidly. There was the brutal "Hanoization" of the south—mass detentions without trial, "re-education" camps, the exile of thousands of people to a harsh life of labor in Siberia. In 1983, Communist Vietnam held as many as 126,000 political prisoners, according to a report by the Human Rights Working Group of the European Parliament. In 1987, according to a Swiss church delegation, 6,000 political prisoners were still held in re-education camps.[15]

If the plight of the people within Vietnam could be ignored, it was all but impossible to deny the tragedy evidenced by the masses of "boat people"—mainly from Vietnam but also from Cambodia and Laos—who were fleeing Communist rule in Indochina. Hundreds of thousands—200,000 in 1979 alone—bore witness to the horror. Other thousands died at sea.[16] The "domino theory" of Communist advance in Indochina had become a vivid and brutal reality.

Religious persecution, notably of Catholics and Buddhists, also began to arise in Vietnam. By August 1976, religious freedom had been severely curtailed; hundreds of Catholic priests had been arrested and others harassed.[17] Even many Catholics and Buddhists who had sympathized with the Communists were thrown into the re-education camps. There, a number of Catholic priests died of ill treatment. Whole Christian communities in the Central Highlands were forcibly relocated, and children were wrenched from their parents to be indoctrinated in Marxism.

There are still churches in Vietnam, though they are essentially government show places. Religious leaders, if subservient to the government, are allowed to travel to "peace conferences" abroad. But there is no freedom "to criticize the ruling powers when necessary," which the Nairobi Assembly of the WCC in December 1975 recognized as "the right and duty of religious bodies."

The WCC has remained silent on these abuses. When in September 1976 a trial of fourteen dissidents ended in death sentences for three of the defendants—one was a Roman Catholic priest—the WCC made not a murmur.[18] On the contrary, addressing the Sixth General Assembly of the Christian Conference of Asia in 1977, WCC General Secretary Potter praised the Vietnamese: "The experience of the Vietnamese people has inspired all who fight for their liberation. The victory of the Vietnamese ended thirty years of the most destructive war the world has ever seen. The most dramatic manifestation of the hope of our time was given by the Vietnamese people."[19]

The entire situation in Indochina was skirted in *Structures of Injustice and Struggles for Liberation* (see Appendix D), a document of the 1975 Nairobi Assembly. An amendment that called attention to "the one-party states in the People's Republic of China, North Korea, Vietnam, Cambodia, and Laos" as being "among the governments violating human rights"[20] was squashed by those (notably Metropolitan Paulos Mar Gregorios of India) who saw no harm in a one-party state.

The amendment was redrafted. It listed the many changes taking place in Asia: "There is martial law in Taiwan; crisis government in the Philippines; emergency rule in India and South Korea; military rule in India and South Korea; military rule in Bangladesh; one-party states in such countries as the People's Republic of China." The amendment continued: "In all the other countries of Asia (for example, Malaysia, Singapore, Australia, New Zealand, Indonesia, and Japan) there are also violations of human rights." References to Vietnam, Laos, and Cambodia—all under Communist domination—were left out of the final text adopted by the Assembly despite these further words in the amendment: "Whenever human rights are suppressed or violated by any Asian government, churches have a duty to work for the defense of human rights, especially of the oppressed."[21]

Earlier, in 1973, the WCC's "Salvation Today" Conference at Bangkok, Thailand, had linked "salvation" to the "peace of the people in Vietnam."[22] Now that there was Communist-imposed "peace" in Vietnam, did this meet the WCC's definition of "salvation"?

The Agony of Cambodia

The WCC was equally evasive about Cambodia. At its Central Committee meeting in August 1986 it avoided making a public statement about the region's deteriorating human rights situation. Reports of mass killings in Cambodia had circulated throughout the West, and had troubled both Western governments and the secular news media, particularly in Europe. Potter's embarrassment at these reports edged him close to incoherence during a press conference shortly before the Committee convened. "The question is not whether or not any Cambodians have been killed," Potter said, "but how one could create the proper atmosphere in order to raise issues through 'person contact.' There is too much self-righteousness on such issues. We should first of all take our own situation into account. We are all sinners."[23] Potter had not been so defensive about American bombing in Vietnam a few years earlier.

The WCC further excused itself for its silence about the Cambodian massacres by pointing to the sparseness of Christian churches in that country. Spokesmen said that the Council "is not a human rights organization, neither does it make statements merely for the purpose of improving its own image."[24] But after Hanoi had installed a sympathetic regime in Phnom Penh, and revealed even more of the atrocities committed in Cambodia by the previous regime between 1975 and 1978, the WCC began to sit up and take notice. Nothing had changed, really, except that the Vietnamese wished to justify their own armed intervention.

The preponderance of evidence suggests that WCC policy toward Indochina was motivated less by humanitarian concerns than by sympathy with certain political regimes. Such evidence continues to accumulate. At the request of the Central Committee, the Council's Commission on International Affairs in 1979 wrote a booklet on the Indochina conflict. It described the post-1975 period in Indochina "as one of consolidation and intensive reconstruction," a view virtually indistinguishable from the official stance of the Communist Vietnamese, who stressed "socialist solidarity" and the need for rapid reconstruction under Hanoi's control. The same WCC that was to denounce American intervention in Grenada in 1984 as a violation of international law made no public statement condemning the Vietnamese intervention in Cambodia. A WCC delegation visiting Vietnam, Laos, and Cambodia in January 1981 concluded that "if all roads in Indochina now lead to Hanoi, that is more by force of circumstances and pressure from countries outside the region than by any deliberate plans for an Indochina federation."[25] Once again, the Soviet-backed Communist regime in Hanoi emerged unscathed from WCC review.

Indochina Refugees

Indochina had a refugee problem even before the Communist takeovers in 1975. To deal with the problem, in 1972 the WCC's Commission on Inter-church Aid, Refugee, and World Service created a special "Fund for Reconstruction and Reconciliation in Indochina." The Fund had a pro-Hanoi bias. At its first major ecumenical consultation in February 1975, it attacked alleged U.S. and South Vietnamese violations of the Paris Agreement on refugees, but ignored similar charges against North Vietnam.

After 1975, the refugee problem took a dramatic turn for the worse, and by 1979 it had reached such vast proportions that Potter sent a message to Kurt Waldheim, U.N. general secretary, requesting help for Indochina's desperate people. Presumably preoccupied by the refugees' plight, Potter never felt compelled to acknowledge that North Vietnam had contributed to the disaster.

Potter also urged WCC member churches to pressure their governments, especially in affluent countries, to accept more refugees from Indochina.[26] Similarly, the 1981 Dresden Central Committee meeting adopted a statement on the "World Refugee Crisis." But still, no government was held culpable for the mass emigration from Indochina.

WCC staff members did not hesitate to name the culprits in other refugee situations. At the Dresden meeting, Alan Matheson, WCC migration secretary, castigated the governments he held responsible for "the other boat people"—the Haitians who were fleeing their homeland. This "tragedy in the history of the oppressed people of Haiti" was caused, Matheson said, by "the cynicism of the United States government, the brutality of some Caribbean governments, the oppression of the Duvalier dictatorship, together with the apathy of the world community."[27]

Communist Vietnam never heard such blunt language from the WCC, whose aid to Indochina was not limited to refugees. WCC assistance was also given to "development projects" in Laos, Vietnam, and Cambodia, and thus helped to consolidate Vietnamese power in the region. The personal ties between Vietnamese government officials, the WCC, and several mainline American Protestant churches in these relief efforts made criticism all the more difficult.

The relief and refugee problem in Cambodia (Kampuchea) is likely to persist into the 1990s. In April 1987, a government statement in Stockholm warned Hanoi that Sweden would halt its aid of $50 million a year to Vietnam if the Communist regime failed to respect its pledge to withdraw its troops from Cambodia by 1990.[28]

CHAPTER SEVEN

The Economic Question

DOMESTIC AND INTERNATIONAL economic problems are inescapably intertwined with politics and national security. All societies face the perplexing problems of how to produce and distribute goods and service. And all governments—democratic, authoritarian, or totalitarian—must decide whether their needs can best be served by a market economy, a centrally administered economy, or a mix of the two. Many Third World countries are in the grip of a modified feudal system under which a small middle class stands between the few very wealthy and the many poor.

In the international sphere, the three principal economic actors are governments, corporations, and financial institutions. The industrial economies of North America, Western Europe, and East Asia trade with and invest in one another and the developing economies of the Third World. There are trade wars, protectionist pressures, and balance of payments and international debt problems. In pursuing their political and economic aims, the Western democracies have encouraged Third World economic development by trade, aid, loans, and investment through bilateral and multilateral arrangements.

There are two general approaches to the economic question. One emphasizes a more immediate, pragmatic, and problem-solving method. The other emphasizes fidelity to an ideology—a worldview—that seeks to explain what is wrong with an existing system and how it could be improved or replaced. The Soviet Union and other Marxist regimes take an ideological approach and practice state capitalism, that is, a centrally controlled and regulated economy. In contrast, most Western industrial states take a pragmatic approach and follow a modified version of democratic capitalism that emphasizes a relatively free interaction of market forces with limited governmental intervention.

For the past decade and more, the leaders of the World Council of Churches have addressed selective aspects of the economic question, almost exclusively from an ideological perspective that asserts the superiority of a government-administered economy over the market. The Council's pronouncements assume a cause-effect relationship between Western capitalism and imperialism on the one hand, and poverty, oppression, and militarism on the other.

In its report "Struggling for Justice and Human Dignity," the WCC Assembly in 1983 condemned Western capitalism as the major source of "injustice in the prevailing economic order" operating "mainly through trade, finance, manufacturing, food processing" and "transnational corporations. . . . The consequences are . . . immense human suffering, degradation, and death."[1] The report added: "Power elites concentrate wealth for the control of political and economic instruments and institutions," and this "*class domination* based on economic exploitation" and the "profit motive" leads to sexism, racism, "cultural captivity, colonialism, and neocolonialism."

This broad and imprecise language captures both the spirit and substance of WCC statements on the economic question since the Nairobi Assembly in 1975. Generally the Council has focused on the alleged evils of capitalism and criticized multinational corporations as instruments of a privileged elite that seeks to exploit and dominate the poor. To meet this problem, the WCC has advocated the creation of a New International Economic Order to bridge the gap between the rich and poor and redistribute the world's resources.

Critique of Capitalism

The Vancouver report cited above declared that the international capitalist system, defined vaguely as "economic domination and unjust social structures," suppresses the "socio-economic rights of people, such as the basic needs of families, communities, and the rights of workers."[2]

As early as 1977 the WCC urged Christians to fight against economic oppression by "mobilizing public opinion" and "exerting pressure on centers of [economic] power."[3] The emphasis was not on charitable aid to the needy, but on a radical restructuring of the world economic system.[4]

The Vancouver Assembly called on the churches to "resist oppressive powers" and act "in solidarity with those who build up people's power designed to shape a more participatory society. . . . International networks of support, facilitated by the churches, should be strengthened and widened. Churches are called to . . . take risks in the search for a new society."[5]

The WCC's pronouncements on capitalism make no mention of the high productivity and other benefits to both developed and developing countries of market enterprise. Nor was any statistical or even anecdotal evidence cited to reinforce the WCC's insistence that free-market capitalism is uniquely responsible for human suffering.

Multinational Corporations

Multinational corporations (MNCs) operate like national firms and seek to maximize profits. A 1982 WCC report on MNCs defined them as "centers of decision—and therefore of power—that operate in more than one country and that plan investment, production, marketing, finance, and prices on a transnational scale; collectively, they are the main agent of transnationalization of the development model characteristic of the industrialized West."[6] The MNCs are, therefore, the "agents" of the oppressive capitalist system.

A report issued by the 1975 Nairobi Assembly argued that MNCs invest in the Third World "to take advantage of the cheap labor," and that the products of that labor were "designed to satisfy the needs of an elite class."[7] The WCC has been especially opposed to MNC operations in South Africa. The Council rejected arguments that corporate investments there promote political and social reform, particularly of Pretoria's apartheid policy, and has consistently supported drives for divestment and disinvestment. The Council's 1973 report, *Time to Withdraw,* advocated immediate disengagement, a view that has continued ever since.[8]

At Nairobi, the WCC established the "Programme on Transnational Corporations" to consider the "*problems* raised by the existence and activities of transnational corporations."[9] The WCC prefers the term "transnational" to multinational. As Isaiah Frank has pointed out, "the preference for 'transnational' is not merely technical; it also rests on the belief that the term more accurately reflects the quality of 'domination' in the parent-subsidiary relationship."[10] In U.N. deliberations, transnational is also the preferred term. The WCC views this domination by a world-wide capitalist system as the root of much injustice in the world. The implied remedy is a global socialist system.

At the Council's 1977 Central Committee meeting, one delegate, Canon Elliott of the Church of Ireland, argued that the Committee should eschew "wholly negative" comments about MNCs and "give some recognition to the achievements of many of these organizations."[11] His views were ignored. The Committee adopted a statement highly critical of MNCs and called for an immediate effort to promote a New International Economic Order.

The statement argued that "the present order is unjust, discriminatory and disadvantageous to the poor countries" that "contain nearly two-thirds of the world's population." MNCs were specifically identified as the culprits: "for some countries," the statement said, "transnational corporations dominate whole sectors of the economy without adequate control." The principal though unnamed culprit appeared to be American capitalism, though there are many European and Japanese MNCs.

The Council continued its attack against MNCs, but provided no hard evidence for any of its assertions. The 1982 Central Committee meeting said that the question of "whether TNCs could" be held "accountable" could not be resolved and asserted that "the churches certainly had experience of people who were oppressed, exploited or excluded by TNCs."[12] The Committee gave no examples either of general exploitation or of individuals who had been "oppressed" or "excluded" by MNCs.

New International Economic Order

The WCC's solution for the world's "maldistribution of wealth" and oppressive structures has been a New International Economic Order (NIEO). The NIEO proposal originated in the early 1970s in the United Nations, where Third World governments were calling for a global redistribution of resources. It is supported by Moscow. Fidel Castro made this point in an early 1986 speech: "The Soviet Union initiated a kind of Christian relation with Cuba that might be considered the New International Economic Order to which we of the world's underdeveloped countries aspire.''[13] Justice for the WCC did not mean equal opportunity or additional aid to or investment in the Third World, but rather a forced redistribution of income and resources from rich countries to poor ones. A 1977 Central Committee statement noted that "the supporters of the NIEO in the industrialized countries are by and large those who are closer to advocating a just, participatory society than its opponents.''[14]

The redistribution proposals called for "structural rethinking" with target goals, including "ownership, control and allocation of natural resources and economic surplus" and "control over the creation, communication and application of knowledge and technology.''[15] The WCC favored a form of international socialism, with what might be termed the "worker countries" taking over the means of production. It made no attempt to specify the alleged evils of the capitalist system, nor did it outline in any detail what the New International Economic Order would entail. But Jan Pronk, a U.N. and WCC economic advisor, has referred to the NIEO as "international democratic socialism.''[16]

Poverty is the plight of all primitive and traditional peoples. Not until the rise of democratic capitalism did any society have the capacity to eliminate stark poverty. Ironically, capitalism, which owes so much to the Protestant work ethic, has become the favorite whipping boy of the WCC's liberation theologians.

The Council position on the world economic situation is a version of "dependency theory." Based on a largely Marxist-inspired economic model, this theory asserts that the Third World is exploited for the economic gain of the industrialized world. Many, perhaps most, economists now find this theory's analysis and conclusions to be seriously flawed.[17]

The Presbyterian Report

In 1983 a remarkably balanced treatment of multinational corporations and international economic development was produced by the United Presbyterian Church in the United States. Written by a Presbyterian Task Force on TNCs, the report realistically assessed the problems and the possibilities of transnational enterprise. It called for a "commitment to reform and improve rather than to destroy and replace" the international capitalist system.[18] Its analysis and recommendations assume the legitimacy of democratic capitalism. The report made no demands for an immediate redistribution of the means of production. It admitted that "the church's witness in economic affairs has frequently suffered from an overemphasis on the negative aspects of corporate and governmental policy." It argued that "the church must be willing to examine its own character and behavior as a transnational corporation by the same rigorous criteria it applies to the economic transnational corporation."

While the report was not produced by the WCC, it appeared to have an impact on subsequent Council pronouncements. The 1984 Central Committee meeting in Geneva expressed concern that high technology was concentrated in the developed countries, but its conclusions were moderate and supported by factual evidence—for example, it noted that "97 percent of global research and development" was undertaken in developed countries.[19] It expressed special solidarity with the "oppressed" poor against established economic elites and called on member churches to allocate specific portions of their budgets to relief efforts.[20]

The WCC Central Committee evidenced a similar restraint on economic issues at its 1985 meeting in Buenos Aires, especially on the international debt crisis. Though advocating such radical measures as outright cancellation of Third World debt in some cases, the Committee concluded that "the present debt crisis forces the poor to bear the burden of debts which were not incurred for their benefit."[21] This can be taken as a criticism of the economic policies of Third World regimes. The WCC analysis was relatively straightforward and reasoned. Also significant was the Committee's emphasis on reform of the debt-payment process, as opposed to social or political revolution as a remedy for the crisis.

The Committee's statement on the international distribution of food was also comparatively restrained. Though still calling for "major political and economic changes," the Committee endorsed essentially conventional recommendations: "the application of appropriate agricultural policies," an alteration in "the emphasis on export-oriented food production" in developed countries, and an analysis of the causes of "the unequal distribution of land."[22]

This trend toward moderation was also evident in the WCC's 1986 Annual Report, *One World*. Its section on "economics and people" avoided a blanket condemnation of capitalism. It focused instead on specific issues such as unemployment and poverty. The report even included a self-critical statement from the head of the Council's Development Committee, Rob van Drimmelen, who admitted that the Council, while "good at criticizing the status quo," does not "offer a thorough analysis of the way things are or suggest strategies for change."[23]

From the 1970s until 1983, the WCC's economic position was overwhelmingly anti-capitalist, anti-market, and anti-multinational corporation. The Council chose to ignore the widespread human misery that real-world socialism had brought about in the Soviet Union, the post–World War II poverty in Communist China, the tragedy of Communist Vietnam, and the economic malaise in Eastern Europe, to say nothing of the disastrous performance of centrally administered economies in the Third World. The remarkable achievements of capitalism in raising living standards in countries like Taiwan, South Korea, and Singapore were also overlooked.

In the wake of the 1983 Presbyterian report, which criticized American churches for their one-sided, anti-capitalist economic stance, the WCC's public statements moderated, though its positions on South Africa, the MNCs, and the New International Economic Order were not officially changed. Calls for revolution gave way to recommendations of realistic efforts to remedy income inequities.

But this moderation appears to have been short-lived. In March 1987, the WCC co-sponsored a consultation to determine whether economic justice is a "confessional" issue, that is, "one on which a person's position determines whether or not he or she stands within the fellowship of the church."[24] The consultation's report declares that "economic-scientific analyses demonstrate that the capitalist system" is "the root cause" of the "reality of poverty, powerlessness, and death imposed on the majority of the world's people." The consultation concluded that it is a "fundamental requirement" of Christian faith to "reject and resist" the current world economic system.[25]

Although the consultation report is not an official WCC pronouncement, it reflects the Council's growing reliance on "center-periphery analysis"—a return to dependency theory under a new name. According to this analysis, transnational corporations are "the infrastructure of neo-colonialism," and the international capital lending system is a "global casino" with "center countries extracting output from periphery countries" and "the International Monetary Fund as 'enforcer' of the rules of the casino."[26] The WCC's Commission on the Churches'

Participation in Development echoes earlier Council statements on how to approach the economic question: "We use a methodology which is biased in the sense that priority is given to listening to the voices of the poor, the oppressed, and the 'sinned-against.' "[27]

CHAPTER EIGHT

Religion in the Soviet Bloc

THE REPRESSION OF believers, churches, and religion itself within the Soviet Union is a profound domestic problem, but it is also an international issue. This is true not only because Moscow is a signatory to various international human rights documents, including the Helsinki Accords of 1975, but because the Soviet Union is officially an atheistic state. The USSR has expressed its ideology and expanded its empire by open military force, economic measures, disinformation, and covert action, to the detriment of other countries and peoples. At home and abroad Moscow uses Russian Orthodox Church leaders for political purposes and employs KGB agents to infiltrate religious organizations. In addition, the Kremlin has drawn an iron curtain around the contiguous Soviet bloc and its client states that seriously restricts emigration for religious or other reasons. The repression and political exploitation of religion within the Soviet Union has been carefully documented by Keston College, a respected research institution near London. Several other groups provide additional information.[1]

From its beginning, the World Council of Churches has insisted that "the right to religious freedom . . . is inseparable from other fundamental human rights," as the Council declared in its 1975 Nairobi Assembly report on *Structures of Injustice and Struggles for Liberation*. (See Appendix D.) The report defined religious freedom as "the freedom to have or adopt a religion or belief of one's choice, and freedom, either individually or in community with others in public or private, to manifest one's religion or belief in worship, observance, practice, and teaching." The report went on to say: "Religious freedom should also

63

include the right and duty of religious bodies to criticize the ruling powers.''

The issue was raised in an unusual way at both the Nairobi and the Vancouver assembly—not through the customary channel of a WCC staff-drafted pronouncement for consideration, but by two Russian Orthodox Christians at Nairobi and by two unofficial letters addressed to the delegates at Vancouver. In both cases, the WCC delegates were urged to grapple with the issue of persecuted Christians in the Soviet Union.

Yakunin-Regelson Affair, 1975

At the Nairobi Assembly in 1975, two Russian Orthodox Christians, not official delegates, issued an "Appeal for WCC Action on Behalf of Persecuted Christians" that was published in *Target,* the daily Assembly newspaper. The signers, Gleb Yakunin, a priest, and Lev Regelson, a layman, charged that "the matter of religious persecution" had been ignored by the WCC and that "it ought to become the central theme of Christian ecumenism."[2] This struck at the heart of a dichotomy in WCC behavior toward the Soviet Union and the West. The Council has repeatedly declined to protest religious repression and human rights violations in the Soviet bloc while rarely hesitating to admonish countries sympathetic with the West. Many delegates at Nairobi were uncomfortable with this selective indignation. Jacques Rossel of Switzerland, for example, was applauded when he proposed that a statement on "Disarmament, the Helsinki Agreement and Religious Liberty" be amended to include the following: "The WCC is concerned about restrictions to religious liberty, particularly in the USSR. The Assembly respectfully requests the government of the USSR to implement effectively principle No. 7 ["Respect for human rights and fundamental freedoms, including the freedom of thought, conscience, religion, or belief"] of the Helsinki Agreement."[3]

In the debate that ensued, Metropolitan Yuvenali, a Russian Orthodox delegate, charged that Rossel's proposal offended Christian charity. A fellow delegate, Metropolitan Nikodim, objected on the grounds of insufficient evidence. In a substitute amendment, Canadian Anglican Archbishop Edward W. Scott recommended that the WCC should say that, while it was "grateful for the leadership" of the USSR in developing "the Helsinki Agreement," the WCC called upon the

Soviet Union "and all governments to give full implementation to Section 7" of the agreement.[4] The drafting committee came up with a compromise: "The Assembly recognizes that churches in different parts of Europe are living and working under very different conditions and traditions"—and more to the same effect. One author of the successful compromise, Alexei Buevski of the Russian Orthodox Church, said that it was conceived "in the spirit of brotherly love, mutual understanding, and the spirit of fellowship." Thus a veil was drawn over the repression of religion in the Soviet Union.[5]

The Yakunin-Regelson letter of protest haunted the entire Nairobi proceedings and threatened the election of Metropolitan Nikodim, leader of the Russian delegation, to one of the WCC's seven presidential positions. No one doubted how the Soviet bloc delegates would vote. The thirty Russian Orthodox delegates, the largest single contingent at Nairobi, had been properly instructed by the official Soviet Council for Religious Affairs, and most of the eighty delegates from the Eastern European churches were under Nikodim's control. There was, however, uncertainty about the Third World delegates, who had been shaken by revelations of Soviet religious repression.

The Russians went into action. With the Assembly well under way, delegates, chiefly from the Third World, were invited to a meeting with the leaders of the Christian Peace Conference, a Prague-based front group organized by the Soviet KGB. The Conference leader was candidate Nikodim. The delegates were reminded of the Soviet government's influence, and of foreseeable consequences to the delegates' respective governments, good or bad, of their policy toward Nikodim's nomination. Nikodim was subsequently elected to a WCC presidency with substantial Third World support.[6]

Increasing Soviet Influence

Though successful in some respects, the Russian Orthodox delegates were not pleased with the Nairobi Assembly. They were unhappy with the substitute amendment proposing "that the question of religious liberty be the subject of intensive consultations with the member churches of the signatory states of the Helsinki Agreement."[7]

Aided by the Council for Religious Affairs, a section of the Soviet KGB, the Russian Orthodox leaders continued to protest the Nairobi compromise after the Assembly, but with mixed results. On the one hand, the WCC's 1976 colloquium on the Helsinki Accords held in Montreux, Switzerland, made clear that "condemnation of violations of human rights wherever they are objectively established is an obligation of the churches and should not be confused with unjustified interference."[8] But, at the same time, the Montreux delegates were quick to acknowledge the importance of "Christian-Marxist dialogue" and to condemn continuing "Cold War attitudes"—that is, Western criticism of the Soviet Union—that "contradict the spirit of Helsinki."[9]

In August 1976, the Central Committee discussed the interrelations between human rights and other international issues. In his report on the Montreux colloquium, General Secretary Philip Potter, who had assumed his office in 1972, said that the struggle for human rights and religious freedom could be pursued only along with "other realities," such as disarmament and détente, a view propounded repeatedly at ecumenical conferences by Soviet bloc delegates.[10]

Though WCC spokesmen have on occasion acknowledged the selectivity of Council pronouncements about Soviet religious persecution, they have in the main defended their silence on the issue by pointing out that repeated criticism of the USSR and its European satellites would jeopardize WCC member churches in those countries. Moreover, they say, information about events in the Soviet bloc is unreliable. For example, Eugene Carson Blake, who was WCC general secretary from 1966 to 1972, argued that "critical concern becomes cheap" and is looked upon "as anti-Communist." Silent diplomacy, he said in 1972, is preferable: "We have often found that such approaches are more successful than public declarations."[11]

That policy was put to the test in November 1979 when the Soviet government arrested Father Yakunin for "anti-Soviet agitation and propaganda." The Moscow Patriarchate of the Russian Orthodox Church did nothing. Father Yakunin was sentenced to five years in prison for slandering the state, to be followed by five years of internal exile. In early 1987 he was released from Siberian exile and appealed to Mikhail Gorbachev to extend his drive for "renewal" to the area of church-state relations.[12] Regelson, the lay co-signer of the letter at Nairobi, was also arrested, but was released after pleading guilty.

The World Council of Churches made no statement on the Yakunin trial.[13] When Michael Bourdeaux, the director of Keston College, called on the Council to declare publicly its support of Yakunin and Regelson, he received a terse reply from Leopoldo Niilus, CCIA director: "Re. Yakunin. At present no action contemplated."

Undeterred, Bourdeaux carried his protest to the British churches and public. "As a result of my challenge to the WCC," Bourdeaux later reported, the Council leaders "wrote to the Russian church expressing their concern about the trials of Christians."[14] That the WCC would, however reluctantly, send such a letter[15] to a Russian Orthodox official was heartening, but the reply of Metropolitan Yuvenali, chairman of the Russian church's Foreign Affairs Department, dampened any optimism. Since "the accused admitted their guilt and showed repentance," he said, "leniency was granted to them in the eyes of the law."[16] Thus, Yuvenali demonstrated that Soviet officials could continue to regard dissidents as criminals for daring to exercise what ought to be a basic freedom.

The Council has continued to justify its selective silence about reports of religious persecution in the Soviet bloc. In 1981, for example, Ninan Koshy of India, who succeeded Leopoldo Niilus as CCIA director, said that the WCC "should not indulge in an ecclesiastical running commentary on world affairs. We have to make a selection and make no apology for it. It is basically the situation of the churches in each country that determines whether our public statements will be effective."[17] A year later, another spokesman explained why the "poor and oppressed" of Nicaragua, Cuba, and Vietnam received significantly more sympathy from WCC pronouncements than did the "poor and oppressed" in the USSR and Eastern Europe:

> To be sure, the Council has never claimed neutrality; after all, the Gospel which it seeks to express is biased in favor of those who have least and suffer most. When you survey the WCC's one hundred plus statements in the seven years since the Nairobi Assembly, you can see that there has clearly been no attempt to even up issues and areas. Statements on human rights and repression outnumber those on doctrinal theology and unity. Appeals for emergency relief outnumber calls for interfaith dialogue. Africa is addressed more often than Eastern Europe.[18]

During the 1970s and early 1980s, the atmosphere in WCC circles on Soviet behavior toward religious activity became more friendly. The number of Eastern Europeans on the Council staff increased, and the number of WCC-sponsored meetings held in Soviet bloc countries also increased. Equally important was an agreement made in January 1980 that gave Soviet bloc churches a greater hand in planning the 1983 Vancouver Assembly than they had had in preparing for the Nairobi Assembly in 1975.

Vladimir Rusak's Open Letter

When the Sixth Assembly convened in Vancouver on July 24, 1983, the WCC leadership, in one respect at least, acted differently than it had eight years before at Nairobi. It refused to allow discussion of an open letter to the delegates from Vladimir Rusak, a deacon in the Russian Orthodox Church, and another letter on behalf of thirty-five imprisoned Christians and twenty thousand Pentecostal Christians who wanted to emigrate from the Soviet Union.

CCIA director Koshy explained the new policy at a press conference: "Appeals from groups or individuals for World Council of Churches intervention cannot be acted on by the Assembly without the support of delegates or member churches, but will be followed up by the WCC general secretary."[19]

In his letter, Rusak charged that "the Soviet authorities" used the church in a "purely propagandistic" way. "It helps increase the political dividends reaped by the authorities on the international scene" and is the reason for "the continued existence of the church in a socialistic state. . . ." The "international activity of our church's representatives," the deacon continued, "is directed, first and foremost, to serve the interests of the secular regime to the detriment of the interests of the church and all the faithful."

Rusak urged the WCC to cease identifying "the Soviet delegation at international gatherings with the whole body of the Russian Orthodox Church" and to "stop treating the propagandistic claims of Soviet delegates as the only source of information." Rusak also urged that religious freedom be discussed openly. The Yakunin-Regelson letter at the Nairobi Assembly, he wrote, had "yielded some definite results." As evidence, he cited "hurried publication of the Bible [in the Soviet Union] which had been awaited by millions of believers for many years," but the number actually printed was severely limited.[20]

Previously, Rusak had been dismissed from his position as deacon by leaders of his church when he refused to destroy a report he had prepared on the history of the Russian Orthodox Church after the 1917 Revolution. The KGB confiscated the report, but not before a copy had been smuggled to the West. In that report, Rusak maintained that the Soviet government deliberately kept the Soviet people uninformed of the real condition of the church: "Obviously, it is easier to manage an ignorant mass of people than an informed one."

The instructions to the WCC staff at Vancouver not to publish the

Rusak and Pentecostal letters were probably due to the furor at Nairobi caused by the Yakunin-Regelson letter. In his statement to the press, Koshy appeared to have articulated Council thinking on human rights violations—that is, not to address those committed by the Soviet government. In March 1982, Koshy himself had sent a telegram to President Ferdinand Marcos of the Philippines protesting the Marcos government's arrest of several Christians.[21]

This apparent double standard surfaced often at Vancouver. The WCC issued, for example, a broad call for church vigilance on behalf of human rights: it is "imperative that member churches and the WCC continue to identify and denounce gross violations of religious freedom and extend moral and material assistance to those who suffer oppression and even persecution because of their religious beliefs and practices."[22] This statement appeared in the Assembly's lengthy "Statement on Human Rights," which also noted that "many persons, including Christians and their leaders, have been imprisoned, tortured, or have lost their lives in service to God and humanity." It goes even further, asserting that "the violations of human rights in many parts of the world have become more widespread and severe," and chiding churches that "have not done enough to counter the forces of evil and death, at times even being in complicity with them." The thrust of this statement could easily be construed as a rebuke to the Soviet bloc governments.

But the Assembly proceeded effectively to undercut any such interpretation: "We have also come to appreciate more clearly the complexity and inter-relatedness of human rights. In this regard we recognize the need to set individual rights and their violation in the context of society and its social structures. We are increasingly aware . . . that human rights cannot be dealt with in isolation from the larger issues of peace, justice, militarism, disarmament, and development."[23]

By reference to "the complexity and inter-relatedness of human rights," any proposed Council action on human rights questions can be smothered in endless discussions of peripheral social, economic, and political issues. By adopting this concept, assiduously promoted by Moscow, the WCC again demonstrated its unwillingness to confront the question of religious repression in the Soviet Union and in countries under its control.

In sum, over the years from the Nairobi Assembly in 1975 through 1986, there was a very small minority of WCC delegates that wanted to acknowledge and condemn religious repression in the Soviet bloc, but this small voice was snuffed out by majority votes of WCC bodies and by leaders of the Council who were determined to suppress or ignore the fact of Communist religious persecution.

CHAPTER NINE

A Revolutionary Stance

BEFORE EVALUATING THE political relevance and moral wisdom of World Council of Churches positions on key international issues, let us review the Council's advice to individual Christians, churches, and governments noted in the foregoing chapters. This advice spans the twelve years from the 1975 Nairobi Assembly to early 1987, including the 1983 Vancouver Assembly. On all major issues, the Vancouver Assembly reaffirmed the pronouncements made at Nairobi and subsequent statements by the Council's Central Committee, which in turn strongly reflected positions taken in several WCC-sponsored conferences and the views of the Council's senior staff and publications. There were no significant differences, for example, between the findings of the WCC Consultation on Militarism held in Glion, Switzerland, in 1977, WCC publications, and Vancouver's position on nuclear arms. The reader should be reminded of the difficulty of discerning operational policy advice because of the vague, ambiguous, and often fragmented character of many pronouncements. (See discussion of this problem in Chapter 1, page 12.)

Nuclear Arms

The WCC insists that Western capitalism and the profit motive are major causes of militarism and war. The U.S. "military-industrial complex" threatens to provoke nuclear war. NATO's doctrine of deterrence—a cluster of policies designed to prevent war—is called "as unmitigated an evil as an actual war," though at one point the WCC conceded that deterrence may provide "interim assurance of peace."

The WCC condemned NATO's deployment of medium-range Per-

71

shing II and cruise missiles to counter the much more powerful and longer-range Soviet SS-20s already in place. There was no specific condemnation of the SS-20s, the Soviet Union's significant tank and short-range missile superiority, or the general build-up of the offensively deployed Warsaw Pact forces. The WCC called the U.S. "neutron bomb" (actually an enhanced radiation warhead) a "dehumanizing weapon" that fueled the arms race, but failed to mention that it was more precise, discriminating, and humane than the weapons it was designed to replace. The Council opposed the U.S. Strategic Defense Initiative and supported all of Chairman Gorbachev's arms control proposals. The posture, advice, and wording of WCC statements on nuclear arms throughout the period closely paralleled that of the secular nuclear freeze movement and other peace campaigns that were supported directly and indirectly by the Soviet Union.[1]

Central America

To put the matter in the briefest and starkest terms, the WCC saw promise and hope in a pro-Soviet Nicaragua moving toward a totalitarian state, and saw impending disaster in a pro-Western El Salvador moving toward democracy. No WCC statement ever praised totalitarianism as such, but many statements supported policies pursued by the Soviet Union. The Sandinistas' increasing repression of Nicaraguan Indians, churches, and human rights generally was downplayed, overlooked, or even justified. Abuses by Salvadoran armed forces were roundly condemned, but those by Salvadoran leftist guerrillas were ignored or excused. The WCC called on external powers not to intervene militarily in Central America, but named only the United States as the culprit. Washington was portrayed as the sole oppressor and exploiter in the region and as the chief barrier to "the forces of historic change." (See Appendix B.)

The Council did not acknowledge that other Central American states were targets of Marxist Nicaragua, supported by massive aid from Cuba and the Soviet Union. In 1983–85, Soviet bloc aid to Cuba and Nicaragua totaled $15.85 billion, while U.S. aid to all of Central America was $3.14 billion. By December 1984, Moscow was providing ten times as much military aid to Nicaragua and Cuba as Washington was to all of Latin America. From 1982 to 1987, Soviet military assistance to the Sandinistas approximated $1 billion, including $600 million in 1986. In 1986, Washington appropriated no military aid to the Nicaraguan democratic resistance, but it allocated $70 million for 1987.

The WCC made no mention of these facts, and insisted on viewing the Sandinistas as the vanguard in the struggle to liberate the region from U.S. repression, imperialism, and capitalism.

Afghanistan

The WCC's resolutions echoed Moscow's view on the Soviet invasion and occupation of Afghanistan and on the conditions for the withdrawal of these forces. The WCC acknowledged the suffering of the Afghan people, but refrained from naming the USSR as the cause. In a strange twist, Council statements tended to put the blame for continuing conflict on the United States for assisting the Afghan freedom fighters. Like Moscow spokesmen, the Council attempted to link Soviet behavior in Afghanistan with the deployment of U.S. missiles in Western Europe. The Vancouver Assembly supported Moscow's two chief conditions for withdrawing its troops: U.S. arms aid to the Afghan resistance must cease, and there must be an agreement between Moscow and the Soviet puppet regime in Kabul. (See Appendix A.)

Southern Africa

According to the WCC, racism, like militarism, is largely a product of Western capitalism and imperialism. The Republic of South Africa was seen as the world's chief racist regime. The Council focused almost exclusively on white racism, rooted in "the self-interest, greed, and values of the 'white' world." In 1979, the Central Committee asserted that "racism of *white people*" was "the most dangerous and powerful" variety and must be "combatted more urgently than any other form of racism or ethnocentrism."[2] This made it awkward for the WCC to condemn injustices against Soviet Jews, Sandinista abuses of Miskito Indians in Nicaragua, or black racism and tribal brutality in many parts of Africa.

The WCC's campaign against white racism around the world has been underwritten by contributions of more than six million dollars (see Appendixes E and F), most of it given to revolutionary groups attempting to overthrow the regime in South Africa by violence and terror, or to maintain in power black Marxist regimes in southern Africa. Since 1970, the Council through the Special Fund of its Program to Combat Racism has contributed $1,348,500 to the South-West African People's Organization (SWAPO), a Soviet-financed and -armed guerrilla group attempting to fight its way to power in Namibia. In the same period, the WCC has contributed $754,500 to the African National Congress (ANC), a terrorist organization supported by the Soviet Union and the Communist Party of South Africa.[3] The ultimate aim of the ANC's core leaders is to install a Marxist regime in Pretoria. Does anyone believe that such a regime in South Africa would be more attentive to a wide range of human rights or more effective in economic development than the present imperfect government or one that would evolve by peaceful means? If we consult the recent record of Marxist regimes in Europe, Asia, Africa, and Latin America, the answer is clear.

East Asia and the Pacific

The WCC's stance toward East Asia is similar to its policy in Central America and Afghanistan—pro-Soviet regimes tend to be exonerated from wrongdoing, while pro-Western governments are singled out for censure. Many elements within the Council saw in Peking's Communist regime a model society and a noble experiment; a few even compared Maoism with the Kingdom of God. The brutality of the Cultural Revolution became a WCC concern only after the fact. The Council did not speak up for the persecuted dissidents in the PRC, but only for dissidents in non-Communist Asian states, particularly in South Korea and in the Republic of China on Taiwan.

The partially democratic Republic of Korea in the south, not the repressive Communist regime in North Korea, took the brunt of the WCC's criticism for human rights abuses.

The Council was also critical of infringements on human rights during the Marcos regime in the Philippines. It condemned the presence of U.S. military facilities in that country, but not the Soviet military bases and presence in Vietnam and Laos, nor Soviet political and military support of North Korea. It made no mention of Soviet-supported Communist guerrillas seeking to overthrow the Manila government of Marcos and later of Aquino.

In the years immediately before the fall of Saigon in 1975, the WCC was more critical of the United States and South Vietnam than of the Soviet Union and the Hanoi regime, which were seeking to take over South Vietnam by force. The Council refused to acknowledge that Hanoi had had any hand in devastating Indochina, but censured the U.S. presence "in any form" in Vietnam as "detrimental to the peace." For the WCC, the United States, not the North Vietnamese Communists who for more than a decade sought to conquer the south, was the oppressor if not the aggressor.

As Hanoi, with Moscow's support, tightened its grip over Vietnam after 1975, human rights were massively violated. Religious persecution, brutal "re-education" camps, and ideological regimentation drove hundreds of thousands of "boat people" to risk their lives for freedom. The WCC remained silent on all these atrocities. But its general secretary, Philip Potter, in 1977 praised the Communist victory in Vietnam as the "most dramatic manifestation of hope of our time." A statement adopted by the Nairobi Assembly in 1975 denounced human rights violations in many Asian countries, including India, Japan, Australia, New Zealand, Singapore, Taiwan, the Philippines, and the People's Republic of China. Strangely, Vietnam, Laos, and Cambodia were not mentioned. After a protracted silence, the WCC finally acknowledged the monstrous genocide of the Pol Pot regime in Cambodia (now Kampuchea).

The Economic Question

The thrust of WCC pronouncements from 1975 until early 1987 was strongly anti-capitalist, anti-market, and supportive of centrally administered economies such as were advocated by Marxist theorists and politicians. The Vancouver Assembly in 1983 condemned Western capitalism as the major source of injustice in the world and multinational corporations as the major vehicle of repression in the Third World. Capitalist corporations rooted in greed and the profit motive lead, the Assembly declared, to sexism, racism, "cultural captivity, colonialism, and neocolonialism."

The remedy for the evils of capitalism with its "maldistribution of wealth" and oppressive structures is, according to the Council, a New

International Economic Order that would transfer resources from the developed countries to the underdeveloped world, really a form of global socialism that focused on distribution rather than on production.

A remarkable 1983 report by the United Presbyterian Church in the United States, though not a part of the ecumenical dialogue as such, apparently had the effect of moderating subsequent WCC statements on the economic question. In essence, the report saw some merit in the market system and called for reforming rather than abolishing the international capitalist system or multinational corporations. The 1984 WCC Central Committee expressed solidarity with the "oppressed" against established economic interests, but noted that "97 percent of global research and development" took place in industrial countries. The Committee in 1985, addressing the international debt issue, acknowledged that the problem was not wholly the fault of the lending countries and institutions and placed some blame on Third World governments. It also called for "appropriate agricultural policies" and change in "export-oriented food production" in developing countries. The WCC's 1986 annual report sidestepped a general condemnation of capitalism and focused on specific issues. In short, the tone of Council statements had moved at least temporarily from demands for radical change to calls for substantial reform.

Religion in the Soviet Bloc

Neither the top WCC staff nor the majority of delegates at the Nairobi and Vancouver assemblies were prepared to deal openly or courageously with religious persecution in the Soviet Union. Though the Council is committed to human rights, especially religious freedom, the staff and most delegates have a record of appeasing the Russian Orthodox Church delegates, who on several occasions have threatened to walk out of the WCC if their government is subjected to the kind of criticism that the WCC so freely bestows on the West, particularly on the United States.

After debating the religious freedom issue, the Nairobi Assembly adopted a compromise resolution that did not mention religious repression in the Soviet Union, but said blandly that the "Assembly recognizes that churches in different parts of Europe are living and working under very different conditions and traditions." The long Human Rights statement at Vancouver acknowledged that many "Christians and their leaders have been imprisoned, tortured, or have lost their lives in service to God and humanity," adding that the churches "have not done enough to counter the forces of evil" and have been "in complicity" with those forces. This could be construed as a rebuke to the Soviet Union, but the Assembly promptly undercut this interpretation by once again tying human rights to "the larger issues of peace, justice, militarism, disarmament, and development," issues on which the United States was deemed the prime offender. This Soviet-sponsored obfuscation insured the defeat of a small minority of delegates who wanted to acknowledge and condemn Communist religious repression.

CHAPTER TEN

A Persistent Double Standard

IN SPITE OF THE confusion and superficiality of the World
Council of Churches' analysis and advice on the international issues
examined in this study, there was rough underlying consistency rooted
in a shared revolutionary worldview. The term WCC, as noted in
Chapter 1, is used to embrace all levels of Council authority from the
Assembly and Central Committee to the seven concurrent presidents,
the secretary general, and the Geneva headquarters staff. All of these
voices spoke with a rare degree of harmony, though there were often
small minorities opposed to what they regarded as a persistent inclination to support, condone, or apologize for Soviet policies or the
denial of freedom and other human rights violations by Soviet-supported regimes in Asia, Africa, or Central America.

From a rational Western perspective, the WCC was using a rubber
yardstick or invoking a double standard, but the matter is more
complex. The Council denounced alleged curbs on religious freedom
in the Philippines and refused to condemn documented and massive
repression of religion in the Soviet Union. According to Western
reason and the rule of law, such behavior is a perfect example of the
double standard. But from the vantage point of revolutionary logic,
including "liberation theology," any action that promotes liberation
(read: revolution) is right and that which impedes it is wrong. During
the past twelve or more years the WCC generally invoked the single
standard of revolutionary logic, having abandoned the canons of social
and political responsibility proclaimed at the 1948 Amsterdam Assembly (see Appendix C). If we assess WCC behavior by the Amsterdam
understanding of the Christian moral tradition, Council leaders have

strayed far from the founders' intention. Egregious examples of how far include the WCC's unwillingness to condemn the Soviet invasion of Afghanistan or to criticize openly religious persecution in the USSR and its praise of the repressive Marxist regime in Nicaragua and condemnation of the democratically elected government in El Salvador.

Unwilling to invoke openly and consistently a Marxist worldview or to advocate openly a Marxist-Leninist solution, General Secretary Potter, the Soviet delegates, and those who made common cause with them found devious devices to achieve the same objective. One such device was the invocation of a "moral symmetry" that equated the real sins of the Soviet Union with the imputed sins of the United States. Hence, Soviet atrocities in Afghanistan were equated with NATO's deployment of Pershing II missiles in Western Europe to counter the much larger, more destructive, and more numerous Soviet SS-20s already in place.

References to religious repression were blunted by the insistence that all human rights must be considered in the light of the larger revolutionary struggle. According to that view, the United States, profit-hungry capitalists, multinational corporations, and Western imperialism generally were responsible for the greatest injustices, especially in the Third World, where these forces were charged with promoting oppression and racism. Repeatedly, the Soviet view of human rights was put forward—the insistence on "economic and social rights" (i.e., employment and health care) as opposed to political and individual rights (i.e., freedom of speech, religion, assembly, and movement). In short, the WCC condemned the West in a vicious circle of vices. If a person or government was guilty of any vice—"white racism," oppression, capitalism, or militarism—he or it was assumed to be guilty of all. This seamless garment of imputed guilt was used repeatedly to denounce the West and to exonerate the Soviet Union.

In sum, the cast of heroes and villains promulgated by the World Council was virtually indistinguishable from that of the propaganda and disinformation spokesmen in Moscow and Havana. It was a kind of George Orwell's *Animal Farm* updated. In Central America, U.S. military aid was severely condemned, Soviet military support of Cuba and Nicaragua was never condemned. Everywhere democratic capitalism was bad, but centrally controlled Marxist economies were good.

Throughout this period, the WCC wittingly or unwittingly advanced long-range Soviet propaganda themes or short-range disinformation issues, such as the promotion of a nuclear freeze. Active measures and disinformation activities sponsored by the Soviet KGB go beyond ordinary propaganda and include the widespread use of front groups, forgeries, smear campaigns, influential persons, organizations in the West, and international agencies such as the World Council of Churches.[1]

The moral dichotomy that favored the Soviet worldview and opposed the democratic West was not always cast in clear and sharp terms, and the various resolutions and preachments were not always internally consistent, or consistent with one another. But the World Council's view of international problems—from nuclear arms to southern Africa—was informed by a revolutionary perspective and driven by a fervor similar to but not as disciplined as the Marxist-Leninist line espoused by the Soviet Union.

Does this mean that the WCC staff in Geneva and other key Council leaders were taking orders from Moscow? Hardly. There has been, of course, increasing Soviet influence, even pressure, on Council deliberations at every level since the Russian Orthodox Church was admitted to membership in 1961. The 100-plus Soviet bloc delegates at Nairobi and Vancouver, along with Third World and Western sympathizers, were very active both in the open and behind closed doors. Evidence suggests that the leading Soviet delegates were under strict orders to push the Soviet worldview and prescription on all key issues. WCC leaders were aware of this. They were also aware that each Russian Orthodox delegation included at least one KGB agent. "Of course we know that," said the late Cynthia Wedel, a former North American president of the Council, to this writer, adding that it was far better to have Soviet delegates in the WCC than outside.

The USSR was also successful in increasing the number of the Soviet and Soviet bloc staffers at the WCC Geneva headquarters, where key policy decisions on the international agenda are made. In a real sense, the development of the World Council of Churches parallels that of the United Nations General Assembly and Secretariat. In both institutions the influence of the Soviet bloc states and their Third World friends has dramatically increased since the 1950s, when Western members could command a majority vote on any important issue. Now, through coalition politics based on the number of member states, a Soviet–Third World alliance can insure a majority vote. At Vancouver, as noted in Chapter 1, there were 336 delegates from the West, compared to 511 from the Soviet bloc and the Third World. At Nairobi, there were approximately 300 Western delegates and 350 from the Soviet bloc and the Third World. Generally, most delegates from Asia, Africa, and Latin America supported the Soviet view along with many from Western countries.[2]

Triumph of Liberation Theology

No simple "devil theory of history" takes into account the reality of multiple causation. The geographical distribution of Assembly delegations alone cannot explain the WCC's revolutionary stance, which came to flower before the 1975 Nairobi Assembly and has flourished ever since. After all, the U.S. National Council of Churches, which has no Soviet or Third World member denominations takes positions almost identical to those of the WCC. In both cases, the councils have been profoundly influenced by the canons of "liberation theology" developed by Gustavo Gutiérrez, a Peruvian Catholic priest, in his book *A Theology of Liberation*, published in 1973. He and other liberationists differ somewhat among themselves, but in essence liberation theology as understood by Catholic and Protestant adherents alike is an operational doctrine that ties Christian salvation to liberation from political repression and economic bondage in this world. In practical terms, this doctrine calls for a class struggle against feudalism, multinational corporations, and Western imperialism along the lines of V. I. Lenin's pregnant dictum: "Imperialism is the last stage of capitalism." As such, liberation theology identifies itself closely with the Marxist-Leninist doctrine and practice of "national liberation," which insists that unjust political and economic structures (capitalism and imperialism) can be eliminated only by protracted pressure, including revolutionary violence.

Opponents of liberation theology regard it as a heresy because it tends to link Jesus Christ with Marx and Lenin and to overlook or distort the transcendent dimensions of the Christian faith. Advocates and critics agree that the liberationist strategy of class conflict is radically different from the Western concept of gradual, peaceful, and democratic movement toward greater justice, freedom, and respect for human dignity. This is not the place to elaborate on liberation theology. Readers interested in the pros and cons of this issue have ample resources available to them.[3]

The WCC has nurtured liberation theology because its Geneva staff,

other Council leaders, and ecumenical Protestant spokesmen believe
that the Marxist-Leninist interpretation of history and its call for
radical change is a relevant and timely answer to the Gospel's demand
for salvation. How can we account for this marriage of Marx and
Christ? Why have many Western leaders of the ecumenical movement
accepted an operational code that in significant ways runs counter to
democratic principles, practices, and successful experience? Why have
they embraced centrally administered economies at the very time when
overwhelming empirical evidence has demonstrated that democratic
capitalism can produce and distribute goods and services far more
effectively and efficiently than either feudal or socialist economies?[4]

This rejection of traditional Western values, including to a significant
extent the Judeo-Christian moral heritage in which they are rooted,
characterized radical politics in America from the mid-1960s to the late
1970s. There is a growing body of thoughtful literature on the rise of
radicalism in the United States and Western Europe.[5] This radicalism
expressed itself in many secular organizations, notably the Institute
for Policy Studies in Washington, D.C.,[6] and in religious organizations,
especially the National Council of Churches. Again, why?

There is no simple answer, but it is a fact that many "new left"
spokesmen were influenced by their sense of guilt over the wealth,
power, and influence of the United States, and ironically by the success
of democratic capitalism in the face of the failed economies of Marxist
states and the persistence of feudal and mercantile practices in many
Third World countries. They tended to blame Third World poverty on
American prosperity and Third World weakness on American power.
They sought to find devils responsible for the material disparities
between the rich and the poor, and the powerful and the weak, and
they fixed on "profit-hungry multinationals" and the market system
itself. A feeling of guilt can be a constructive emotion leading to
compassion and a humane quest for bread, peace, justice, and freedom. But an inordinate and misplaced sense of guilt can lead to
demands for a "new order" with little rational concern for what the
new order may bring. It can manifest itself in a kind of naive utopianism
that can be exploited by the hard-headed and committed utopians in
their ruthless drive for power.

Strong idealistic, even utopian, hopes are a part of the American
character, along with the vaunted American pragmatism. Many American intellectuals want to believe that mankind is perfectible, and that
progress in history is not only possible but inevitable if only we rid

ourselves of greed, the urge to dominate others, and militarism. This utopianism is often expressed in a kind of perverse American anti-Americanism, an attitude one sees in the writings of a Richard J. Barnett[7] or a Garry Wills, in which the real United States—its society, culture, economy, political system, and foreign policy—fails to measure up to the author's vaguely articulated ideals. In his review of *Reagan's America: Innocents at Home* by Wills, published in 1987, Irving Kristol says the book is "an indictment of Ronald Reagan, of the American people who elected him, of the American history that shaped him and them. It is an act of revenge by a homeless sophisticate against all those innocents at home in America. Garry Wills no doubt considers himself a patriotic American, but it is a patriotism directed toward some ideal, never existing, still-to-be-born America."[8] Many American ecumenical leaders are afflicted by this strange alienation against what is properly called mainstream America.

Most American idealists are "soft utopians," as Reinhold Niebuhr has called them. They believe in the efficacy of love, good will, and education in solving the world's perplexity and conflict. Thus, they often become easy marks for the "hard utopians"—that is, the Marxists who insist that noble aspirations are futile unless they are enlisted in a violent class struggle. These Marxists are quite prepared to assert that Marxism is the champion of the world's poor, oppressed, and exploited peoples, though fewer today insist that the Soviet Union is the foremost model.

Truth and Consequences

The big truth is that Marxism as an ideology and Leninism as an operational code have failed miserably to usher in a new and better age. The dream of Marx and Lenin has become a nightmare.[9] In the Soviet Union and in all other places it has been tried, Marxism has led to repression, tyranny, and continued—and often worsened—poverty. But in one important respect the Soviet Union has been highly successful. It has mastered the techniques required to gain and maintain power by an ambitious and disciplined elite. These techniques range from raw military force to exquisite brain-washing and disinformation techniques. Perhaps the chief attraction of the Soviet Union or the "totalitarian temptation," as it has been called, to Third World leaders or would-be leaders is precisely the Soviet capacity to install, prop up, and direct new power elites. How else can we explain a Fidel Castro in Cuba, a Mengistu Haile Mariam in Ethiopia, or an Agostimbo Neto in Angola?

What, then, are the consequences of this truth, this failure of Marxism, for the liberation theologians and the World Council leaders who have become so infatuated with this idolatrous secular utopianism? The consequences are catastrophic. If Marxism in theory and practice has failed, those closely associated with it have failed or will fail. If, for example, the WCC's moral and material support of the ANC, SWAPO, and the Pan Africanist Congress of Azania (PAC) in southern Africa helps these Soviet-supported terrorist groups to install Marxist regimes in Namibia and South Africa, will not the WCC have to share with Moscow the blame for the evil consequences that will follow? Herman Nickel, then the Washington editor of *Fortune,* said in 1979 that "liberation theology embraced by the WCC draws attention to one of the least attractive features of a self-indulgent age: the attempt to expiate past 'sins' by supporting policies whose burden in bloodshed and human misery must be borne by others."[10]

One cannot easily divine the true motives of individuals or complex organizations when they express compassion for the oppressed or outrage against the real or supposed oppressor. But certainly the desire to "expiate past 'sins,' " or to feel good regardless of consequences, cannot be ruled out. This politics of sentiment, rather than of reason and responsibility, recalls the idealistic school teacher in the British play *The Prime of Miss Jean Brodie,* who sent her star pupil to participate in the Spanish Civil War; not until the girl's tragic death did the compassionate teacher know on which side her pupil had fought. Miss Jean Brodie never understood the moral or political dimensions of that struggle.

Christian ethics is concerned with ends (they must be just), means (they must be appropriate), and consequences (they should advance just ends). By this measure, the WCC's "advice" on international issues, if it were taken seriously by Western political leaders, would lead to a disaster for the cause of freedom and human dignity. Fortunately, the World Council of Churches is seldom taken seriously. Most consequential religious, academic, political, and business leaders have long since recognized the irresponsibility of the WCC's advice.

The real tragedy of the WCC's flawed witness to the world is not that statesmen ignore what the Council says, but that the Council has failed its member churches and the millions of Christian citizens who belong to them. When speaking to the churches, the WCC has failed to instruct them adequately about the real issues in a dangerous world, the agonizing decisions that confront statesmen, and the limited choices that citizens have. It has presented a highly skewed picture of reality, one distorted by the bankrupt ideology and practice of Marxism.

Further, its analysis and advice have been both superficial and often morally wrong because the WCC ignored or sold short the rich moral heritage of the Judeo-Christian tradition. In the name of justice, the WCC has supported violent revolution that brings neither justice nor freedom. In the name of peace, the WCC has supported policies that would make war or nuclear blackmail more likely. Peace without freedom or justice is tyranny. George F. Will in his foreword to *Amsterdam to Nairobi* wrote that readers "can decide for themselves the extent to which bad sociology, bad theology, bad faith, and, yes, sin feed on one another and are to blame for what the WCC has been doing."[11]

Fortunately, for the millions of Christians who have a right to expect better from the WCC there are alternative sources of fact, insight, and advice on international problems that are rooted in reality and instructed by a commitment to peace, freedom, justice, and human dignity. I refer to a growing stream of literature from statesmen, scholars, journalists, and theologians that is readily available in books, journals, and newspaper columns. The thoughtful writing of two late theologians come to mind, John Courtney Murray and Reinhold Niebuhr.[12] These and other contemporaries merit mention: P. T. Bauer, Peter L. Berger, Zbigniew Brzezinski, William F. Buckley, Vladimir Bukovsky, Midge Decter, Paul Hollander, Paul Johnson, Jeane Kirkpatrick, Henry A. Kissinger, Charles Krauthammer, Irving Kristol, Clare Boothe Luce, Richard John Neuhaus, Edward Norman, Michael Novak, Cardinal John J. O'Connor, Norman Podhoretz, Paul Ramsey, Aleksandr Solzhenitsyn, and George F. Will. (Many of these authors are listed in the bibliography of this book.) While there is diversity among them, each respects our Western moral tradition and draws heavily on the empirical studies of reliable university, government, and other public policy research institutions. With this wealth of historically grounded and empirically verified information, one is constantly amazed that Christian clergy, academics, and laymen turn to secular ideologues of the extreme left for their understanding of this world.

Future of the WCC

DOES THE WORLD COUNCIL OF CHURCHES have a future?
Does it deserve to have a future? Or has it already passed into a state
of benign ineffectiveness? These are not trivial questions. Let me deal
with the last one first. If the WCC were a dead or dying horse, this
book would have been unnecessary. True, the WCC's approach to
world affairs is not taken seriously by serious statesmen. Nor does its
stance have any discernible impact on the majority of believers in the
churches that belong to it. But it is influential in perverse ways,
primarily as a continuing source of confusion and as an active sup-
porter of revolutionary elites, both religious and secular. Many WCC
leaders participate in international conferences and movements committed to revolutionary and violent change. They are active in a global
network of radical academics, scientists, journalists, and politicians
that provides ideas, training, and money for "liberation" efforts driven
by Marxist-Leninist fervor and frequently supported by the Soviet
Union.

Does the WCC have or deserve to have a future? In my study
*Amsterdam to Nairobi: The World Council of Churches and the Third
World,* published in 1979, I concluded, as I have in the present volume,
that the WCC's political stance since the mid-1960s has been profoundly misguided. Then I harbored the hope that the Council could
be reformed, that it could return to a realistic and non-utopian understanding of the world, recognizing both human limitations and human
possibilities, and thus become an authentic voice of the great Christian
moral tradition for our troubled times.

There is considerable evidence that the earlier book had an impact
in both religious and secular circles. Some WCC critics said the book
"shook the Council to its foundations." This turned out to be an
exaggeration. The book certainly irritated Council stalwarts, but it did
not lead to significant reform.

The modest study, along with the founding of the Institute on Religion and Democracy in 1981 and other developments, did help, however, to precipitate a critical evaluation of both the World Council of Churches and the U.S. National Council of Churches. The results included a revealing CBS-TV "Sixty Minutes" program (January 23, 1983) that exposed a pattern of ecumenical support for violent revolutionary movements. That same month there was also a critical *Reader's Digest* article by Rael Jean Isaac.[1] The Salvation Army withdrew from the WCC and several churches suspended their membership. Countless church members and local congregations in the United States and elsewhere have withheld funds from the WCC or its Program to Combat Racism, the agency that has provided almost seven million dollars to revolutionary causes on four continents.

How have the Geneva headquarters staff and the WCC's policy-making bodies that pronounce on international issues responded to the rising criticism since 1975? It is difficult to give an adequate answer. Certainly there is a mood of greater caution and defensiveness. There have been internal efforts to tighten up policy-making procedures and to institute some cosmetic changes in organization and rhetoric. There is a sign of some moderation in the Council's statements on international economic issues. But in substance, the liberation theology whose triumph was ratified and further nourished at Nairobi is still the reigning doctrine in the Church and Society efforts of the Council. The Faith and Order activities have been only marginally affected. "Given the hostile theological environment of the WCC, its Faith and Order Commission has remained remarkably faithful to the original ecumenical vision," says Lutheran theologian Richard John Neuhaus.[2]

Those within the ecumenical orbit who have worked and prayed for a new beginning—a return to the deeper understanding of the transcendental and the temporal, the dream and reality that brought the World Council into being in 1948 (see Appendix C) and guided it for most of its first two decades—were deeply disappointed when its international stance at Vancouver in 1983 turned out to be little more than a slightly updated replay of Nairobi eight years before. The Council's marching credo still appears to be the Nairobi report, *Structures of Injustice and Struggles for Liberation*. (The full text is found in Appendix D.)

In the concluding observations in *Amsterdam to Nairobi*, I advanced eight suggestions for reforming the World Council to make its social witness politically responsible and true to the deepest Christian moral tradition.[3] These included more disciplined attention to the sources of that tradition: the Old Testament prophets, the teachings of Jesus, and the great theologians from St. Paul and St. Augustine to Reinhold Niebuhr and John Courtney Murray. Also, I urged the WCC to consult the most reliable empirical studies on how constructive change and adaptation actually take place, and at the same time to reject all secular and religious utopian doctrines.

In the area of self-understanding and ecumenical policy, I called upon the WCC to develop a clearer appreciation of the different but complementary functions of church, state, and citizen, and cautioned the Council against presuming to speak *for* the churches when it should be speaking *to* them. To insure more thoughtful debate on complex issues, I suggested that the WCC make a determined effort to provide for greater theological and political diversity within the Geneva staff and in the policy-making bodies, and in general to become more democratic and responsive in its procedures. The senior staff, including the general secretary, should be servants of the Assembly, Central Committee, and Executive Committee, and in no sense the master of these bodies.

Like Paul Ramsey, whose book *Who Speaks for the Church?* was published in 1967, I was critical of the WCC's "passion for numerous particular pronouncements" that reflected a confusion over the proper spheres of church and state, between specialists and ordinary citizens.[4] Carl F. H. Henry, the founding editor of the evangelical fortnightly *Christianity Today,* commended Ramsey for revealing "the worst incursion of churchmen into political affairs since the Middle Ages."[5] Ramsey's advice of two decades ago is still valid:

> It has been easier to arrive at specific recommendations and condemnations after inadequate deliberation than to penetrate to a deeper and deeper level the meaning of Christian responsibility—leaving to the conscience of individuals and groups of individuals both the task and the freedom to arrive at specific conclusions through untrammeled debate about particular social policies. Radical steps need to be taken in ecumenical ethics if ever we are to correct the pretense that we are makers of political policy and get on with our proper task of nourishing, judging, and repairing the moral and political *ethos* of our time. . . . Our quest should be to find out whether there is anything especially Christian and especially important that churchmen *as such* may have to say in the public forum concerning the direction of public policy—not directives for it.[6]

There is little evidence that these suggestions and similar ones by other friendly critics have been taken seriously. With few exceptions, the ideas and procedures of those pursuing a politically revolutionary course in the international arena are still the prevailing ones in Council circles. I hope that radical reform—a return to the principles of the 1948 Assembly—may still be possible, but I see little hope for significant constructive change in the near future. Perhaps some dramatic event will force a thorough reevaluation. I hope so. I respect those who seek to reform the World Council of Churches from within or from without. But I am inclined to look elsewhere in the Christian community for the development and practice of a morally sound and politically responsible approach to the perplexing problems of this world.

In a larger sense, the ecumenical movement as manifest in the WCC and the U.S. National Council of Churches—especially in the past two decades—has failed in its culture-forming mission in the Western world. It should be noted here that the main thrust for creating the modern ecumenical movement came from the dynamic interaction of Protestant pluralism in the United States, symbolized by the establishment of the Federal Council of Churches in 1908 and the International Missionary Council in 1921. The character of ecumenical activities since then has reflected in a large measure the changing theological and ecclesiastical trends in mainline Protestant America. From colonial times until recent years in America, the Protestant tradition has performed well the culture-forming task, including the development of a widely shared political ethic. But since the mid-1960s, as Richard John Neuhaus and others have pointed out, the Protestant mainline has forfeited this crucial culture-forming role out of fatigue, lack of creativity, and self-alienation from the classic Christian moral tradition.[7] Hence, the ecumenical movement's social witness has become obsolescent, marginal, irrelevant, or worse.

Who, then, will move in to fill the moral and political vacuum? Who will provide the spiritual core of Western culture? Who will articulate an authentic political ethic? The answer, I believe, lies in a combination of contemporary forces, including Protestant evangelicals, sectors of the Roman Catholic Church, and leaders of the Lutheran tradition. And certainly conservative elements in American Judaism will make a contribution to the revitalization and renewal of the great Judeo-Christian moral tradition.

My hope is that concerned Protestants will join in fresh efforts to recapture the vision of the 1948 founding WCC Assembly in Amsterdam as expressed in its report, *The Church and the Disorder of Society:*

Men are often disillusioned by finding that changes of particular systems do not bring unqualified good, but fresh evils. New temptations to greed and power arise even in systems more just than those they have replaced because sin is ever present in the human heart. Many, therefore, lapse into apathy, irresponsibility and despair. The Christian faith leaves no room for such despair, being based on the fact that the Kingdom of God is firmly established in Christ and will come by God's act despite all human failure.

APPENDIX A

Resolution on Afghanistan, 1983

This resolution was debated and adopted by the Sixth Assembly of the World Council of Churches, Vancouver, Canada, July 24–August 10, 1983. The text is from Gathered for Life: Official Report, *VI Assembly of the World Council of Churches, edited by David Gill (Grand Rapids: Eerdmans, 1983), pages 161–62.*

The Sixth Assembly recalls the concern regarding the Afghan situation expressed in earlier statements by the World Council of Churches.

We note that the continuing fighting there has led to tremendous suffering for vast sections of the population, many of whom have become refugees. The UN estimates that there are more than three million Afghan refugees in Pakistan and Iran.

We note initiatives, including that of the non-aligned movement, for peaceful resolution of the conflict. We welcome specially the initiatives taken by the Secretary General of the United Nations for resolving the conflict, summarized as follows:

- an end to the supply of arms to the opposition groups from outside;

- creation of a favorable climate for the return of the refugees;

- guarantee of the settlement by the USSR, the USA, People's Republic of China, and Pakistan;

- withdrawal of Soviet troops from Afghanistan in the context of an overall political settlement, including agreement between Afghanistan and the USSR.

We support the Secretary General's current efforts and hope that the negotiations among the parties concerned will lead to a comprehensive settlement.

We believe that this would enable the Afghan people to follow freely their own path of development and to progress towards a more just society. We also believe that such an agreement would reduce tension in the region and also contribute to improvement of relations between the USA and USSR and of international relations in general.

Meanwhile, the WCC should continue to provide humanitarian assistance to the Afghan refugees.

91

Statement on Central America, 1983

This statement was debated and adopted by the Sixth Assembly of the World Council of Churches, Vancouver, Canada, July 24– August 10, 1983. The text is from Gathered for Life: Official Report, VI Assembly of the World Council of Churches, *edited by David Gill (Grand Rapids: Eerdmans, 1983), pages 157–60.*

1. Promising signs of life are appearing within Central America. They are like a young plant striving to rise from the earth, yearning to grow and to be a blessing for the world. Thus, Jesus Christ, the life of the world, teaches us, his disciples, that life must be nourished and defended against the powers of death and of oppression which oppose it.

> God remembers those who suffer;
> He does not forget their cry,
> And he punishes those who wrong them.
>
> The needy will not always be neglected;
> The hope of the poor will not be crushed for ever.
> (Ps. 9:12, 18)

2. Central America is caught up in an agonizing struggle to recast the foundations of its peoples' life. The struggle of life confronting death is a daily one. The depth of this struggle—political, economic, ideological, social, cultural, spiritual—is of historic proportions. Grounded in a common history of harsh colonialism, of exploitation of the poor, and of the concentration of power and wealth countries in the region are in different ways under siege.

3. The current United States administration, acting on its perception of the nation's security, has adopted a policy of military, economic, financial, and political initiatives designed to destabilize the Nicaraguan government, renew international support for Guatemala's violent military regimes, resist the forces of historic change in El Salvador, and militarize Honduras in order to insure a base from which to contain the aspirations of the Central American peoples. This policy is publicly articulated as a framework within which objectives of peace, reform, economic development and democracy can be achieved and communism and "export of revolution" prevented.

4. Indeed the opposite prevails: fear and tensions are heightened; scarce resources needed to meet basic human needs are diverted; the chances of war, potentially devastating to Central America and the Caribbean, escalate; and, in the long term, the legitimate interests and security of the nations and peoples of the American hemisphere are threatened. There can be no security in the region without fidelity to the persistent, yearning struggle of the Central American peoples for peace with justice.

5. International price declines in the region's key export crops have severely strained the region's economies, further exacerbating political, economic and social tensions. Adding to these economic problems, the United States administration has successfully harnessed international financial institutions to its Central American strategy.

6. In this context, the churches, endeavouring to respond to the needs of the region's suffering population, are also having to face the divisive effects of an aggressive new wave of mainly US based and financed religious groups. They are a source of great concern to the churches, particularly as these groups appear, in the churches' analysis, to be used for political purposes in legitimizing policies of repression.

7. Guatemala in the past year has witnessed massacres of civilian non-combatant populations, a large number of extrajudicial executions and the extermination of thousands of people among the Indian population in ways which defy belief. Despite the magnitude of economic, political and military resources provided to the regime by the United States, the El Salvadoran government has demonstrated an inability to curb human rights violations and implement needed reform. The Legal Aid Christian Service, of the Roman Catholic Archdiocese of San Salvador, reports a number of over 2,000 civilians and non-combatants who have been executed outside the law during the period running from January to April of this year, by members of the armed forces, by paramilitary organizations and by death squads for political reasons. The policies of the Honduran government threaten the territorial sovereignty of Nicaragua and cause considerable harassment to refugees from El Salvador. Churches report severe human rights violations committed by intelligence and security forces. Other countries—such as Belize, Costa Rica and Panama—have been the object of pressures brought to bear upon them so as to affect events within Guatemala, El Salvador, Honduras and Nicaragua.

8. Refugees, displaced persons and divided families are a powerful testimony to the bloodshed and terror perpetrated on the poorest of the region's people. Approximately 500,000 human beings have been forced to flee their country and one million more have been displaced from their homes in Guatemala alone. El Salvadoran refugees in Honduras and Guatemalan refugees in southern Mexico continue to be vulnerable to incursions by military forces into camps.

9. In the context of the theme of the Sixth Assembly, "Jesus Christ—the Life of the World," and given the escalation of aggressive acts against Nicaragua, we lift up our concern for the people of the entire region by drawing attention to the life-affirming achievements of the Nicaraguan people and its leadership since 1979. Noteworthy was the decision of the government to abolish the death penalty and to release several thousand members of Somoza's National Guard. In

addition, an internationally-acclaimed literacy programme, the eradication of poliomyelitis and reduction of malaria, an effective land reform scheme and significant progress in constitutional development, preparatory to holding elections in 1985, have helped to give concrete expression to the region's aspirations. The government has demonstrated its openness in acknowledging the inappropriateness of some policies related to the Miskito Indian and other ethnic groups of the Atlantic Coast, and is moving towards reconciliation. It is also important to note that the Nicaraguan process has involved the full participation of Christians, both Roman Catholic and Protestant, at every level of reconstruction and nation-building.

10. This life-affirming process is having to confront death on a daily basis. The United States–financed former National Guard, now based in Honduras, have thus far claimed 700 lives, mainly Nicaraguan young people who are members of the volunteer militia. Tensions with Honduras have escalated dangerously. Nicaragua's call for bilateral talks with Honduras has failed. In the interest of peace, Nicaragua has now indicated its willingness to enter multilateral talks. However, United States support for the former National Guardsmen continues and the Reagan administration, pleading peace and dialogue, takes steps to assemble weaponry and support troops in Honduras and to deploy naval vessels off both Nicaraguan coasts.

11. Nicaragua's destabilization is an affront to life and is fully capable of plunging not only the countries of Central America but also those of the Caribbean into deeper suffering and widespread loss of life. It undercuts the legitimate call and struggle of the poor throughout the region for an end to exploitation and for an opportunity to determine their own path on the difficult pilgrimage of those who seek to enjoy life in all its fullness.

12. The Sixth Assembly affirms the right of the Central American peoples to seek and to nourish life in all its dimensions. It therefore:

   i) *Expresses* to the Central American churches the profound concern and solidarity of the worldwide ecumenical community, as Christian sisters and brothers experience and respond to the critical threats to life, reiterating its strong commitment to the churches' witness, ministries and presence. It commends the Nicaraguan Christian community for its active participation in the building up of national institutions and reconciliatory processes leading to peace with justice;

  ii) *Vigorously opposes* any type of military intervention by the United States, covert or overt, or by any other government in the Central American region. The Assembly commends the churches in the United States for their prophetic expressions of the condemnation of such intervention, and calls upon them to intensify their efforts to press for a radical change of US policy in the region. It urges member churches in other countries to make strong representations to their governments so as to press the United States administration to reverse its military policies, as a positive step towards the building of peace in the region;

 iii) *Calls upon* the new government of Guatemala to reverse the policies of repression by which large numbers of its population have been exterminated and to take immediate steps to restore respect for human rights;

iv) *Urges* the government of El Salvador to enter into a fruitful process of dialogue with representatives of its political and military opposition, so as to bring long-lasting peace to the country;

v) *Calls upon* the churches and the ecumenical community to throw their full weight into supporting peace initiatives, such as that of the "Contadora" group of Latin American states;

vi) *Encourages* the churches in Central America to redouble their efforts to gather and communicate, to the worldwide ecumenical community and other international constituencies, information on the developing critical situation affecting the region, as long as it is necessary;

vii) *Affirms* and *encourages* the process of reconciliation among Nicaraguan minorities and the Spanish-speaking majority and urges the Nicaraguan government to maintain its openness and commitment to increasing the sensitivity of its policy and practice in this area.

The Church and the Disorder of Society
A Report from the Amsterdam Assembly of the World Council of Churches, 1948

This report more than any other adopted by the Inaugural Assembly of the WCC deals with social and political issues related to the Third World. It was received by the Assembly and commended to the churches for their "serious consideration and appropriate action." The text is from First Assembly of the World Council of Churches: Amsterdam, Holland, August 22nd–September 4th, 1948 *(Geneva, Switzerland: World Council of Churches, 1948), pages 39-47.*

I. THE DISORDER OF SOCIETY

The world today is experiencing a social crisis of unparalled proportions. The deepest root of that disorder is the refusal of men to see and admit that their responsibility to God stands over and above their loyalty to any earthly community and their obedience to any worldly power. Our modern society, in which religious tradition and family life have been weakened, and which is for the most part secular in its outlook, underestimates both the depth of evil in human nature and the full height of freedom and dignity in the children of God.

The Christian Church approaches the disorder of our society with faith in the Lordship of Jesus Christ. In Him God has established His Kingdom and its gates stand open for all who will enter. Their lives belong to God with a certainty that no disorder of society can destroy, and on them is laid the duty to seek God's Kingdom and His righteousness.

In the light of that Kingdom, with its judgment and mercy, Christians are conscious of the sins which corrupt human communities and institutions in every age, but they are also assured of the final victory over all sin and death through Christ. It is He who has bidden us pray that God's Kingdom may come and His will may be done on earth as it is in heaven; and our obedience to that command requires that we seek in every age to overcome the specific disorders which aggravate the perennial evil in human society, and that we search out the means of securing their elimination or control.

97

Men are often disillusioned by finding that changes of particular systems do not bring unqualified good, but fresh evils. New temptations to greed and power arise even in systems more just than those they have replaced because sin is ever present in the human heart. Many, therefore, lapse into apathy, irresponsibility and despair. The Christian faith leaves no room for such despair, being based on the fact that the Kingdom of God is firmly established in Christ and will come by God's act despite all human failure.

Two chief factors contribute to the crisis of our age. One of these is the vast concentrations of power—which are under capitalism mainly economic and under communism both economic and political. In such conditions, social evil is manifest on the largest scale not only in the greed, pride, and cruelty of persons and groups; but also in the momentum or inertia of huge organizations of men, which diminish their ability to act as moral and accountable beings. To find ways of realizing personal responsibility for collective action in the large aggregations of power in modern society is a task which has not yet been undertaken seriously.

The second factor is that society, as a whole dominated as it is by technics, is likewise more controlled by a momentum of its own than in previous periods. While it enables men the better to use nature, it has the possibilities of destruction, both through war and through the undermining of the natural foundations of society in family, neighborhood and craft. It has collected men into great industrial cities and has deprived many societies of those forms of association in which men can grow most fully as persons. It has accentuated the tendency in men to waste God's gift to them in the soil and in other natural resources.

On the other hand, technical developments have relieved men and women of much drudgery and poverty, and are still capable of doing more. There is a limit to what they can do in this direction. Large parts of the world, however, are far from that limit. Justice demands that the inhabitants of Asia and Africa, for instance, should have benefits of more machine production. They may learn to avoid the mechanization of life and the other dangers of an unbalanced economy which impair the social health of the older industrial peoples. Technical progress also provides channels of communication and interdependence which can be aids to fellowship, though closer contact may also produce friction.

There is no inescapable necessity for society to succumb to undirected developments of technology, and the Christian Church has an urgent responsibility today to help men to achieve fuller personal life within the technical society.

In doing so, the Churches should not forget to what extent they themselves have contributed to the very evils which they are tempted to blame wholly on the secularism of society. While they have raised up many Christians who have taken the lead in movements of reform, and while many of them have come to see in a fresh way the relevance of their faith to the problems of society, and the imperative obligations thus laid upon them, they share responsibility for the contemporary disorder. Our churches have often given religious sanction to the special privileges of dominant classes, races and political groups, and so they have been obstacles to changes necessary in the interests of social justice and political freedom. They have often concentrated on a purely spiritual or other-worldly or individualistic interpretation of their message and their responsibility. They have often failed to understand the forces which have shaped society around them, and so they have been unprepared to deal creatively with new problems as they have arisen in technical civilization; they have often neglected the effects of industrialization on agricultural communities.

II. ECONOMIC AND POLITICAL ORGANIZATION

In the industrial revolution economic activity was freed from previous social controls and outgrew its modest place in human life. It created the vast network of financial, commercial and industrial relations which we know as the capitalist order. In all parts of the world new controls have in various degrees been put upon the free play of economic forces, but there are economic necessities which no political system can afford to defy. In our days for instance, the need for stability in the value of money, for creation of capital and for incentives in production, is inescapable and world-wide. Justice, however, demands that economic activities be subordinated to social ends. It is intolerable that vast millions of people be exposed to insecurity, hunger and frustration by periodic inflation or depression.

The Church cannot resolve the debate between those who feel that the primary solution is to socialize the means of production, and those who fear that such a course will merely lead to new and inordinate combinations of political and economic power, culminating finally in an omnicompetent State. In the light of the Christian understanding of man we must, however, say to the advocates of socialization that the institution of property is not the root of the corruption of human nature. We must equally say to the defenders of existing property relations that ownership is not an unconditional right; it must, therefore, be preserved, curtailed or distributed in accordance with the requirements of justice.

On the one hand we must vindicate the supremacy of persons over purely technical considerations by subordinating all economic processes and cherished rights to the needs of the community as a whole. On the other hand, we must preserve the possibility of a satisfying life for "little men in big societies." We must prevent abuse of authority and keep open as wide a sphere as possible in which men can have direct and responsible relations with each other as persons.

Coherent and purposeful ordering of society has now become a major necessity. Here governments have responsibilities which they must not shirk. But centres of initiative in economic life must be so encouraged as to avoid placing too great a burden upon centralized judgment and decision. To achieve religious, cultural, economic, social and other ends it is of vital importance that society should have a rich variety of smaller forms of community, in local government, within industrial organizations, including trade unions, through the development of public corporations and through voluntary associations. By such means it is possible to prevent an undue centralization of power in modern, technically organized communities, and thus escape the perils of tyranny while avoiding the dangers of anarchy.

III.   THE RESPONSIBLE SOCIETY

Man is created and called to be a free being, responsible to God and his neighbour. Any tendencies in State and society depriving man of the possibility of acting responsibly are a denial of God's intention for man and His work of salvation. A responsible society is one where freedom is the freedom of men who acknowledge responsibility to justice and public order, and where those who hold political authority or economic power are responsible for its exercise to God and the people whose welfare is affected by it.

Man must never be made a mere means for political or economic ends. Man is not made for the State but the State for man. Man is not made for production, but production for man. For a society to be responsible under modern conditions it is required that the people have freedom to control, to criticize and to change their governments, that power be made responsible by law and tradition, and be distributed as widely as possible through the whole community. It is required that economic justice and provision of equality of opportunity be established for all the members of society.

We therefore condemn:

1. Any attempt to limit the freedom of the Church to witness to its Lord and His design for mankind and any attempt to impair the freedom of men to obey God and to act according to conscience, for those freedoms are implied in man's responsibility before God;

2. Any denial to man of an opportunity to participate in the shaping of society, for this is a duty implied in man's responsibility towards his neighbour;

3. Any attempt to prevent men from learning and spreading the truth.

IV.   COMMUNISM AND CAPITALISM

Christians should ask why communism in its modern totalitarian form makes so strong an appeal to great masses of people in many parts of the world. They should recognize the hand of God in the revolt of multitudes against injustice that gives communism much of its strength. They should seek to recapture for the Church the original Christian solidarity with the world's distressed people, not to curb their aspirations towards justice, but, on the contrary, to go beyond them and direct them towards the only road which does not lead to a blank wall, obedience to God's will and His justice. Christians should realize that for many, especially for many young men and women, communism seems to stand for a vision of human equality and universal brotherhood for which they were prepared by Christian influences. Christians who are beneficiaries of capitalism should try to see the world as it appears to many who know themselves excluded from its privileges and who see in communism a means of deliverance from poverty and insecurity. All should understand that the proclamation of racial equality by communists and their support of the cause of colonial peoples makes a strong appeal to the populations of Asia and Africa and to racial minorities elsewhere. It is a great human tragedy that so much that is good in the motives and aspirations of many communists and of those whose sympathies they win has been transformed into a force that engenders new forms of injustice and oppression, and that what is true in communist criticism should be used to give convincing power to untrustworthy propaganda.

Christians should recognize with contrition that many churches are involved in the forms of economic injustice and racial discrimination which have created the conditions favourable to the growth of communism, and that the atheism and the anti-religious teaching of communism are in part a reaction to the chequered record of a professedly Christian society. It is one of the most fateful facts in modern history that often the working classes, including tenant farmers, came to believe that the churches were against them or indifferent to their plight. Christians should realize that the Church has often failed to offer to its youth the appeal that can evoke a disciplined, purposeful and sacrificial response, and that in this respect communism has for many filled a moral and psychological vacuum.

The points of conflict between Christianity and the atheistic Marxian communism of our day are as follows: (1) the communist promise of what amounts to a complete redemption of man in history; (2) the belief that a particular class by virtue of its role as the bearer of a new order is free from the sins and ambiguities that Christians believe to be characteristic of all human existence; (3) the materialistic and deterministic teachings, however they may be qualified, that are incompatible with belief in God and with the Christian view of man as a person, made in God's image and responsible to Him; (4) the ruthless methods of communists in dealing with their opponents; (5) the demand of the party on its members for an exclusive and unqualified loyalty which belongs only to God, and the coercive politics of communist dictatorship in controlling every aspect of life.

The Church should seek to resist the extension of any system, that not only includes oppressive elements but fails to provide any means by which the victims of oppression may criticize or act to correct it. It is a part of the mission of the Church to raise its voice of protest wherever men are the victims of terror, wherever they are denied such fundamental human rights as the right to be secure against arbitrary arrest, and wherever governments use torture and cruel punishments to intimidate the consciences of men.

The Church should make clear that there are conflicts between Christianity and capitalism. The developments of capitalism vary from country to country and often the exploitation of the workers that was characteristic of early capitalism has been corrected in considerable measure by the influence of trade unions, social legislation and responsible management. But (1) capitalism tends to subordinate what should be the primary task of any economy—the meeting of human needs—to the economic advantages of those who have most power over its institutions. (2) It tends to produce serious inequalities. (3) It has developed a practical form of materialism in western nations in spite of their Christian background, for it has placed the greatest emphasis upon success in making money. (4) It has also kept the people of capitalist countries subject to a kind of fate which has taken the form of such social catastrophes as mass unemployment.

The Christian churches should reject the ideologies of both communism and *laissez faire* capitalism, and should seek to draw men away from the false assumption that these extremes are the only alternatives. Each has made promises which it could not redeem. Communist ideology puts the emphasis upon economic justice, and promises that freedom will come automatically after the completion of the revolution. Capitalism puts the emphasis upon freedom, and promises that justice will follow as a by-product of free enterprise; that, too, is an ideology which has been proved false. It is the responsibility of Christians to seek new, creative solutions which never allow either justice or freedom to destroy the other.

V. THE SOCIAL FUNCTION OF THE CHURCH

The greatest contribution that the Church can make to the renewal of society is for it to be renewed in its own life in faith and obedience to its Lord. Such inner renewal includes a clearer grasp of the meaning of the Gospel for the whole life of men. This renewal must take place both in the larger units of the Church and in the local congregations. The influence of worshipping congregations upon the problems of society is very great when those congregations include people from many social groups. If the Church can overcome the national and social barriers which now divide it, it can help society to overcome those barriers.

This is especially clear in the case of racial distinction. It is here that the Church has failed most lamentably, where it has reflected and then by its example sanctified the racial prejudice that is rampant in the world. And yet it is here that today its guidance concerning what God wills for it is especially clear. It knows that it must call society away from prejudice based upon race or colour and from the practices of discrimination and segregation as denials of justice and human dignity, but it cannot say a convincing word to society unless it takes steps to eliminate these practices from the Christian community because they contradict all that it believes about God's love for all His children.

There are occasions on which the churches, through their councils or through such persons as they may commission to speak on their behalf, should declare directly what they see to be the will of God for the public decisions of the hour. Such guidance will often take the form of warnings against concrete forms of injustice or oppression or social idolatry. They should also point to the main objectives toward which a particular society should move.

One problem is raised by the existence in several countries of Christian political parties. The Church as such should not be identified with any political party, and it must not act as though it were itself a political party. In general, the formation of such parties is hazardous because they easily confuse Christianity with the inherent compromises of politics. They may cut Christians off from the other parties which need the leaven of Christianity, and they may consolidate all who do not share the political principles of the Christian party not only against that party but against Christianity itself. Nevertheless, it may still be desirable in some situations for Christians to organize themselves into a political party for specific objectives, so long as they do not claim that it is the only possible expression of Christian loyalty in the situation.

But the social influence of the Church must come primarily from its influence upon its members through constant teaching and preaching of Christian truth in ways that illuminate the historical conditions in which men live and the problems which they face. The Church can be most effective in society as it inspires its members to ask in a new way what their Christian responsibility is whenever they vote or discharge the duties of public office, whenever they influence public opinion, whenever they make decisions as employers or as workers or in any other vocation to which they may be called. One of the most creative developments in the contemporary Church is the practice of groups of Christians facing much the same problems in their occupations to pray and take counsel together in order to find out what they should do as Christians.

In discussing the social function of the Church, Christians should always remember the great variety of situations in which the Church lives. Nations in which professing Christians are in the majority, nations in which the Church represents only a few per cent of the population, nations in which the Church lives under a hostile and oppressive Government offer very different problems for the Church. It is one of the contributions of the ecumenical experience of recent years that Churches under these contrasting conditions have come not only to appreciate one another's practices, but to learn from one another's failures and achievements and sufferings.

VI. CONCLUSION

There is a great discrepancy between all that has been said here and the possibility of action in many parts of the world. Obedience to God will be possible under all external circumstances, and no one need despair when conditions restrict greatly the area of responsible action. The responsible society of which we have spoken represents, however, the goal for which the churches in all lands must work, to the glory of the one God and Father of all, and looking for the day of God and a new earth, wherein dwelleth righteousness.

Structures of Injustice and Struggles for Liberation

A Report from the Nairobi Assembly of the World Council of Churches, 1975

This was probably the most debated and controversial report adopted by the Fifth Assembly of the WCC. Addressed largely to Third World issues, it is more militant in tone and broader in scope than the Amsterdam Assembly's report on "the disorder of society" twenty-seven years before (see Appendix A). The report as a whole was adopted by a substantial majority of the delegates, and the human-rights amendment (paragraph 81, section 5) was accepted unanimously. Its many recommendations (paragraphs 74-90) were commended to the member churches for appropriate action. The text is from Breaking Barriers: Official Report of the World Council of Churches, Nairobi, 23 November–10 December, 1975, *edited by David M. Paton (London: SPCK, 1975), pages 100-119.*

Preamble

1. Structures of injustice and struggles of liberation pose a formidable challenge to the Church today. In striving to meet it, the Church has no other foundation on which to stand than it has in Jesus Christ. From him it has received its mandate: to witness to the truth which judges and to proclaim the good news which brings about freedom and salvation. In seeking its particular place in today's struggles for social justice and human liberation, the Church needs to be constantly guided by its divine mandate.

2. Whenever a Christian is confronted by structures of injustice and takes part in struggles for liberation, he or she is bound to experience the grip of destructive forces which are at work throughout the human family. Such forces give a taste of the "principalities and powers" of which Paul spoke.

3. The gospel brings us a message of God's total identification with humanity which is suffering under sin and other destructive powers. God's own solidarity with human beings is expressed in the reality of the servant Christ who humbled

himself to take up human form, who was born into poverty, who accepted the path of rejection, and who finally met his death on the cross. The vicarious suffering of Christ is the supreme manifestation of God's love. God in Christ took upon himself the whole burden of human sin and weakness.

4. God calls his Church, a community of forgiven sinners, to follow Christ on the same path committed to the cause of the poor, oppressed, and rejected, to declare the love of God by word and by the whole of life and to accept the cross.

5. The meaning of human suffering in itself is ambiguous. It both reflects the evils which plague the human race and it opens us to God's redeeming activity. In suffering for the cause of justice and for the sake of the gospel, the Church may participate in the vicarious suffering of Christ himself.

6. Is there readiness for suffering in our churches today? Or are our church structures built for our own protection and security and have they therefore become barriers which prevent us from sharing suffering in obedience to Christ and from receiving or reflecting God's redeeming love?

7. Christians who suffer together for the cause of justice and liberation find a deep experience of community with each other and with Christ. This community transcends differences of ideology, class, and Christian tradition. It is knit together by the power of forgiveness and love. It reflects the life of the ultimate community of the Triune God, and the expression of its deepest solidarity with the suffering and sinful humanity is the sharing of the Eucharist.

8. Suffering, however, is not the goal: beyond the cross is the resurrection. Christ has overcome the power of sin and death and broken the grip of the principalities and powers now still seemingly self-reinforcing and outside the control of persons involved. The victory of Christ therefore brings a tangible and deepened hope to those engaged in actual struggles against oppression and dominance. Moreover, his victory promises that the vicious circle in which injustice breeds more injustice and one form of oppression gives way to another form is being broken.

9. We realize that those who operate the structures of oppression are dependent on the people they oppress and that both are equally in need of liberation and God's forgiving love. In this fallen world, however, it is far more likely that the will and strength to end oppression come from those who bear the brunt of it in their own lives rather than from the privileged persons, groups, and nations.

10. Structures of injustice and struggles of liberation cannot be separated from each other. For practical purposes, however, we have divided this Report into three main sections: Human Rights, Sexism, and Racism.

HUMAN RIGHTS

Introduction

11. Our concerns for human rights are based on our conviction that God wills a society in which all can exercise full human rights. All human beings are created in God's image, to be equal, infinitely precious in God's sight and ours. Jesus Christ has bound us to one another by his life, death, and resurrection, so that what concerns one of us concerns us all.

12. Thus God's will and his love are intended for all and the struggle of Christians for human rights is a fundamental response to Jesus Christ. That gospel leads us to become ever more active in identifying and rectifying violations of human rights in our own societies, and to enter into new forms of ecumenical solidarity with Christians elsewhere who are similarly engaged. It leads us into the struggle of the poor and the oppressed both within and outside the Church as they seek to achieve their full human rights, and frees us to work together with people of other faiths or ideologies who share with us a common concern for human dignity.

13. In working for human rights we are often tempted to deal with symptoms rather than root causes. While we must work for the abolition of specific denials of human rights, such as torture, we must remember that unjust social structures, expressed through, e.g., economic exploitation, political manipulation, military power, class domination, psychological conditioning, create the conditions under which human rights are denied. To work for human rights, therefore, also means to work at the most basic level towards a society without unjust structures.

14. In our fallen world, there is no nation where human rights have been fully achieved. Because of discrepancies between what we profess and what we practise it is crucial for the churches to move from making *declarations* about human rights, to working for the full *implementation* of those rights. As Christians we affirm that the gospel brings about a human dignity which transcends our own human potential.

15. The world community has agreed upon certain high principles which are embodied in the Universal Declaration of Human Rights and the International Covenants on Human Rights. The recent Helsinki Declaration on Security and Co-operation in Europe gives, particularly for its signatories, a new potential for the implementation of these standards. These principles and standards largely coincide with our current Christian understanding about what makes up a just society.

16. Our chief task is to work for the realization of these enunciated rights *where we are*, but when there are those elsewhere who are powerless to cry out, we are called to be the voice of the voiceless and the advocates of the oppressed. In order to do this we must base our actions on accurate information. For this, open channels of communication are vitally important.

17. Common to all expressions of human rights is the right to self-determination by individuals, groups, and nations. The balance between these claims is always precarious, and their creative interrelationship may differ in various times and places. A distinction can be made, for example, between the limitation of rights due to all and the limitation of privileges available only to a few. Christians will need to assess different structures carefully, championing the rights of the individual when they are threatened by unjust structures and defending the rights of the majority when they are threatened by the tyranny of the few, and always bearing in mind that rights involve responsibilities.

18. Within this overall framework there are a number of specific human rights to which attention must be directed.

The Right to Basic Guarantees for Life

19. No rights are possible without the basic guarantees for life, including the right to work, to adequate food, to guaranteed health care, to decent housing, and to education for the full development of the human potential. Because women have the lowest status in most world communities their special needs should be recognized.

20. The ever-widening gap between rich and poor nations and between rich and poor within many nations has created today a highly explosive situation in which millions are denied these rights. This is due to a number of contributing factors, including the following:

(a) The present international economic structures are dominated by a few rich countries who control a large proportion of the world's resources and markets.

(b) Transnational corporations, often in league with oppressive regimes, distort and exploit the economies of poor natio 1s.

(c) National economies are controlled in many cases by a small group of elites who also often give special access to transnational corporations.

(d) Patterns of land ownership are often exploitative.

21. The right to the basic guarantees for life involves guarding the rights of future generations, e.g., through protection of the environment and conservation of the earth's resources.

The Rights to Self-Determination and to Cultural Identity, and the Rights of Minorities

22. All people have the right freely to determine their political status and freely to pursue their economic, cultural, and social development. These rights are often violated by foreign governments and power systems, and through internal oppression and discrimination.

23. The churches should condemn such violations and take active part in efforts to ensure national sovereignty and self-determination for people who are deprived of them.

24. The churches must also defend and promote the rights of minorities (including that of migrant workers), be they cultural, linguistic, religious, ideological, or ethnic. Efforts to ensure that the Helsinki declaration be implemented could be of great importance in this context, especially for minorities in countries who have signed it.

25. The churches must closely scrutinize the reasoning of people in power when they seek to justify the violation of human rights for what they deem to be overriding concerns. Even in times of public emergency, fundamental rights such as the right to life and personal dignity, as defined by the Universal Declaration of Human Rights and the Covenants, should under no circumstances be derogated from.

The Right to Participate in Decision-Making within the Community

26. Participation of groups and individuals in the decision-making processes of the various communities in which they live is essential for achieving a truly dem-

ocratic society. As a precondition, there must be created an economic and social foundation which is in the interests of all segments of society. All members of the community, especially the young and women, should be educated in a spirit of social and political participation and responsibility. The structures of government on the national and local levels, within the religious communities, educational institutions, and in employment, must become more responsive to the will of all the persons belonging to these various communities, and must provide for protection against manipulation by powerful interests.

27. Women, because of their particular experience of oppression and the new insights they are receiving in the process of liberation, can often make a special contribution regarding participatory decision-making. They are exploring styles of shared leadership in which power and decision-making is horizontal rather than hierarchical, fluid rather than static. The Church, like the community, needs to receive this contribution, if it is to develop unifying and freeing structures.

28. Churches should participate in developing activity through which local communities of poor people, industrial and rural workers, women, minority groups, and others who suffer from any form of oppression can become aware of their condition and influence the course of the society.

The Right to Dissent

29. The right to dissent preserves a community or system from authoritarian rigidity. It is essential to the vitality of every society that the voices of dissenters be heard and that their right to hold opinions without interference, to freedom of expression, and to peaceful assembly be guaranteed. Christians, as followers of Jesus Christ, have a solidarity with the people who suffer because of their religious faith and practice and because of their stand in favour of political and social justice. Christian solidarity means a definite choice on the side of prisoners of conscience and political prisoners and refugees. The churches should make all efforts in their witness and intercessions, and by providing remedial assistance, to support those fellow human beings who suffer.

30. In readiness to reassess and to change their own structures and attitudes wherever necessary, the churches and the World Council of Churches itself must give all due attention within their communities to men, women, and young people who take a critical stand towards the predominant views and positions of their churches and of the World Council of Churches.

The Right to Personal Dignity

31. In many countries represented in this Section, evidence has been cited of gross violations of the right to personal dignity. Such violations include arbitrary arrest and imprisonment, torture, rape, deportation, child-battering, enforced hospitalization in mental hospitals, threats to families, and denial of habeas corpus. In some cases, prisoners and refugees are denied contact even with their families, thus becoming "non-persons." In other cases, arrested persons either disappear or are executed summarily.

32. The basic causes for these violations are to be found in the unjust social order, the abuse of power, the lack of economic development, and in unequal

development. This leads to violations of unjust laws and rebellion by the dispossessed, to which political and military forces of "law and order" respond with cruel repression. In some cases, the churches themselves have actively supported the oppressors or even become involved in the oppression itself, out of misguided convictions and/or attempts to safeguard their own privileges.

33. We also observe the increasing role, both nationally and internationally, of security police and para-police forces in the violation of the human right to personal dignity.

The Right to Religious Freedom

34. The right to religious freedom has been and continues to be a major concern of member churches and the WCC. However, this right should never be seen as belonging exclusively to the Church. The exercise of religious freedom has not always reflected the great diversity of convictions that exist in the world. This right is inseparable from other fundamental human rights. No religious community should plead for its own religious liberty without active respect and reverence for the faith and basic human rights of others.

35. Religious liberty should never be used to claim privileges. For the Church this right is essential so that it can fulfil its responsibilities which arise out of the Christian faith. Central to these responsibilities is the obligation to serve the whole community.

36. The right to religious freedom has been enshrined in most constitutions as a basic human right. By religious freedom we mean the freedom to have or to adopt a religion or belief of one's choice, and freedom, either individually or in community with others and in public or private, to manifest one's religion or belief in worship, observance, practice, and teaching. Religious freedom should also include the right and duty of religious bodies to criticize the ruling powers when necessary, on the basis of their religious convictions. In this context, it was noted that many Christians in different parts of the world are in prison for reasons of conscience or for political reasons as a result of their seeking to respond to the total demands of the gospel.

Human Rights and Christian Responsibility

37. Churches and other Christian communities carry, on the basis of the gospel, a special responsibility to express in word and deed their solidarity with those people whose human rights and fundamental freedoms are denied.

38. During its deliberations, the Section made frequent reference to the report of the consultation on "Human Rights and Christian Responsibility" held in St. Pölten, Austria, October 1974.

SEXISM

39. For the sake of the unity of the Church and humankind, the concerns of women must be consciously included in every aspect of the deliberations of the WCC. The liberation of women from structures of injustice must be taken seriously as seen in the light of the liberation of all oppressed people and all forms of discrimination.

40. At Amsterdam (1948) it was stated that "The Church, as the Body of Christ, consists of men and women, created as responsible persons to glorify God and to do God's will." Dr. W. A. Visser 't Hooft has added that "this truth, accepted in theory, is too often ignored in practice."

41. Despite efforts of the WCC in the past, the position of women, in both the Church and the world, has not changed significantly. As long as women are largely excluded from decision-making processes, they will be unable to realize a full partnership with men and therefore the Church will be unable to realize its full unity.

We wish to identify three areas in which change is necessary:

The Area of Theology:

42. A thorough examination needs to be made of the biblical and theological assumptions concerning the community of women and men in church and society.

43. Particular attention should be paid to the relationship of cultural assumptions and the way we understand the Word of God. Women and men in the Church are in need of clarification of the various biblical texts relating to the role of women in the story of creation and redemption.

These and other theological dimensions of our faith need to be re-examined, drawing heavily on the investigations of women as well as of theologians and scholars.

44. Language in many instances and the connotations of language in other instances fail to reflect the depth of the mystery of God who transcends all human metaphors and images. It is important that our language about God be inclusive (e.g., Isa. 49.15; 46.3-4; Matt. 23.37) to be true to the original biblical text. As the mother of Jesus, Mary embodies particular significance for Christian women and men. Her openness and willingness to respond to the call of God, in ways which were totally unexpected, proclaim to all people their responsibility to be free from any preconceived understandings as to how God works in and through people.

45. Also, it is important that the member churches of the WCC examine their liturgical language and practices with a view to eliminating sexist patterns so that women may join fully in the worshipping community.

The Area of Participation:

46. In order to be truly free, all people must participate in working towards their own liberation. This can be seen in all struggles for human rights and to overcome oppression.

47. The WCC must recognize the dimensions of powerlessness that affect women in the political, economic, social, and ecclesial areas of life. It should therefore continue its work, the work begun in International Women's Year, in working on the ten-year plan for action.

48. The model for this work should aim at providing funds for self-development and self-help programmes. We draw attention to the following vital areas:

(a) The urgent need to secure water supplies for women who are responsible for obtaining water for their community—in rural situations and others where water is not in easy supply;

(b) the need to facilitate indigenously-based self-help programmes which particularly relate to the needs of women, including the need to educate all women about the importance in all questions concerning their reproduction functions and the rights of their unborn children, and also regarding nutrition;

(c) the need to examine the relationship women hold to the law—both judicial and customary law (e.g. dowry systems), family law, inheritance law, contract and loan law. Women also need to be helped to understand their rights under present legal systems;

(d) the need to recognize that where racism is involved women are the most disadvantaged group of all.

The Area of Relationship:

49. A third area of urgent concern is the interrelationship of women and men who frequently exploit one another. This exploitation often takes the form of misuse of power over each other which is linked with lack of understanding of their mutual identity.

50. People need to feel independent, valuable, and secure in the totality of their identity as men and women before they can relate to each other in mutual interdependence.

51. For this to happen it is essential that women unite in supportive groups to find solidarity with their sisters, and a new sense of worth. Such a discovery of worth is essential for the full development of equal partnership.

52. We recognize that men and women together form one corporate body in Christ and that they cannot be seen in separation from each other; nevertheless, evidence shows that in many marriage relationships women and men are unable to develop their full personhood. The Christian Church is in a key position to foster and support the partners to marriage in their search for mutuality.

53. The Church is in the same unique position in respect to persons living in different life situations (e.g. single people living in isolation, single parents), extended families, and persons living in communal patterns. There is evidence that these people are not fully accepted by many societies and are often ignored by the Church.

54. In the social relationships between women and men, the dynamics that are set up by oppression are such that women have a particular understanding of, and interest in, reconciliation of confrontation and conflict. They are emphatic that those who are liberated from oppression should not become the oppressor in the same structures. This can only prevent true liberation and perpetuate conflict.

55. Recognizing that small advances in the position of women in church and society have been made, we are nevertheless convinced that it is vital for the WCC and the member churches to open all service opportunities to women and to encourage the study, by both men and women, of a deeper and more thorough participation of women in church life with special attention to the question of ordination and the employment of women in the Church.

56. The freedom and unity of Jesus Christ includes both halves of the human community; therefore it is imperative to the unity of church and society that the full participation of women be given urgent consideration and immediate implementation.

RACISM

Fundamental Convictions

57. Racism is a sin against God and against fellow human beings. It is contrary to the justice and the love of God revealed in Jesus Christ. It destroys the human dignity of both the racist and the victim. When practised by Christians it denies the very faith we profess and undoes the credibility of the Church and its witness to Jesus Christ. Therefore, we condemn racism in all its forms both inside and outside the Church.

58. When we again try to deal with racism at this Assembly we cannot but begin by confessing our conscious and unconscious complicity in racism and our failures to eradicate it even from our own house. In previous Assemblies we have many times affirmed as churches our common rejection of racism. Yet, we still find ourselves only at the beginning. We stand in need of God's forgiveness and grace which will free us from our complicity and failures, towards a new commitment, to strive for the justice that will bring an end to all racism.

59. The past years of struggle against racism have shown that we as churches need a more profound understanding of the nature and of all varied manifestations of racism. We need to confront it with the fullness of the biblical message, to see more deeply its demonic character, and also to comprehend its psychological, economic, and social impact on persons and communities and its roots in societies. However, although our understanding needs to grow, we already know more than enough to participate in obedience to Christ in the fight against the manifestations of racism in politics and in the Church.

60. Concerning the methods to be used in the fight against racism, we join the agonizing search for guidelines on how to deal with the inevitable question of violence and non-violence. A helpful contribution to this search has been made in the paper "Violence, Non-violence, and the Struggle for Social Justice" (commended by the WCC Central Committee, 1973).

The Scope of Racism—a Litany of Shame

61. Racism can be seen today in every part of the world. No nation is totally free of it. Its victims cross the paths of most of us daily. Yet, it is obvious that some of our countries are more visibly plagued by it than others, e.g., where racism is legally enforced. We heard in the Section from every continent a series of passionate pleas to draw the common attention of the churches here to the outrageous expressions of racism in their respective countries, like a litany of shame of the whole human family. However, it brought home the growing urgency of the problem of racism on every continent.

62. There is much evidence that racially oppressed communities are rapidly becoming aware of the injustices to which they are subjected and that they more and more refuse to endure indignity and exploitation. Consequently, they are increasingly determined to liberate themselves and thereby affirm their humanity. We need to express our solidarity with them.

63. It also became obvious that racism is a factor in numerous violations of human rights and fundamental freedoms as dealt with in another part of this Report.

Racism in Churches

64. To our shame, Christian churches around the world are all too often infected by racism, overt and covert. Examples of it include the following:

   (a) churches and congregations have been and are still being organized along racially exclusive lines;

   (b) congregations welcome to their fellowship warmly those who are like the majority of its members, but easily reject those who are different;

   (c) many argue that they are free of racism as if its reality could be undone by ignoring it;

   (d) churches frequently contribute to the psychological conditioning of the racially oppressed so that they will not sense the racism imposed upon them;

   (e) they are more willing to support struggles against racism far from home than to face the racism which is practised on their doorstep;

   (f) churches often reflect the racially prejudiced attitudes of their governments, their elites, and self-pretensions, while presuming that their own attitudes arise out of Christian faith;

   (g) in leadership privileges and in programmatic priorities churches tend too easily to indulge in racism without even recognizing it.

65. We recognize that the Spirit of God does break through structural and other barriers so that Christian communities do from time to time rise to challenge their own racism and to seek models of commitment to a non-racist Christian faith, even if for every such sign of hope there remain too many examples of denial.

Institutional Racism

66. Pervasive as individual attitudes and acts of racism may be, the major oppressive racism of our time is imbedded in institutional structures that reinforce and perpetuate themselves, generally to the great advantage of the few and the disadvantage of many. Examples of this:

   (a) racism openly enforced by law;

   (b) predominantly white North Atlantic nations create trade patterns and preferences that militate against other racial groups;

   (c) strong military powers and other industrialized countries supply sophisticated arms and assistance to racist regimes;

   (d) powerful countries, without regard to their social system, often entrench themselves in supporting racial repression under the pretence of legally justified defence of their own national self-interest;

   (e) continued patterns of settler colonialism contribute to racial oppression;

   (f) the powerful in affluence, education, ecclesiastical position, or secular authority, tend to protect their systems of privilege and to shut out of the decision-

making any influence of the weak and the subordinate. Moreover, they tend to overlay their racism privileges all too often with an aura of kindliness and service.

67. Institutionalized racism, in its many structural forms, resists most challenges with careful concessions calculated to preserve its power. We reject a conspiratorial theory of history that oversimplifies the complex struggles of humanity for liberation by describing all institutions with power as pernicious and all powerless peoples as virtuous. This does not, however, make us blind to the evident inclination of current power structures to perpetuate racism. All these institutional forms of racism need to be carefully analysed and as Christians we need to attack them with prophetic word and action.

Interdependence of Oppression

68. We lift up for special attention the fact that across the globe racist structures reinforce each other internationally. Self-serving policies of transnational corporations operate across boundaries with impunity; weapons or mercenaries are supplied internationally to local elites; the worldwide communications networks are manipulated to reinforce racist attitudes and actions. It is precisely because of this world-wide web of racist penetration that the churches must seek out policies and programmes at ecumenical and international levels. Such programmes can expose international systems which support racism and provide an effective counter-response to them.

69 In this connection it should be noted that churches and their foreign mission agencies in the West ought to re-examine their use of human and material resources so that they can effectively support liberation efforts and contribute to human dignity in developing countries in ways that are beyond the scope of traditional patterns of giving and receiving.

70. The multinational character of racist structures also makes necessary a constant vigilance by Christians so that they are ready to speak and act and that the pressure of international challenges to racism is felt and felt strongly, and the victims of racism may know that they are not abandoned and that their liberation is essential to the liberation of all.

The Urgency of the Task of the Churches

71. The grip of racism is today as acute as ever because of its institutional penetration, its reinforcement by military and economic power and because of widespread fear of loss of privilege by the affluent world.

72. This gives a special urgency to the task of the churches both in facing and eradicating racism within themselves and their home countries and in strengthening their international efforts against racism.

73. Southern Africa deserves continued priority in the churches' combined efforts because of the churches' own involvement in the area and because of the legal enforcement of racism there. African delegates brought forcefully before us the need of churches to practise what they preach. What is at stake is the faithfulness to the fullness of the message entrusted to the Church.

RECOMMENDATIONS

ON SEXISM

74. Whereas a thorough examination needs to be made of the biblical and theological assumptions concerning the community of women and men in the Church, *it is recommended that* the WCC shall commend the study document "The Community of Women and Men in the Church" (1975) to its member churches and invite their active participation in a three-year study in which:

1. priority be given to a theological study of sexuality, taking into account the culture of the member churches;

2. women theologians and scholars be invited to participate fully in the study;

3. care be taken in translations of the word of God, which always comes in human language, so that they reflect the gender used in the original language, and to consider developing principles for the elimination of sexist terminology, if any, in our languages.

75. Whereas there is ample evidence that the expertise and gifts of women are not being fully used by any Church, *it is recommended that* the WCC shall urge:

1. member churches to consider making available funds for theological education of women (especially advanced study);

2. member churches to ensure full participation of women in all decision-making bodies;

3. those churches that ordain women to give them the same opportunities and pay as men, according to the measure of their gifts (1 Cor. 12);

4. those member churches which have agreed in principle to the ordination of women to the priesthood/ministry to take immediate action to admit women to all their ordained ministries, taking into serious consideration that there are other churches of our WCC fellowship that are not in agreement with this practice;

5. those member churches which do ordain women and those which do not continue dialogue with each other and with non-member churches about the full participation of women in the full life of the Church including ordained ministries, according to the measure of their gifts.

76. Whereas men and women in some parts of the world are living at subsistence level, while others are living at adequate and more than adequate levels; and whereas women have special responsibilities for bringing new life into the world, nurturing and rearing children, *it is recommended that* the WCC shall urge its member churches and those present at this Assembly to encourage women and men to:

1. realize that all those who benefit from the economic exploitation of other people in any part of the world have to share the responsibility for such exploitation, even if they are not directly involved; and to act to bring pressure on governments, transnational corporations, and other bodies whenever they are oppressive;

2. participate fully in the ecclesial, political, economic, and social structures of their own societies at all levels to change these towards a more just society;

3. help local congregations and communities to study and implement the UN

Ten Point World Plan of Action (cf. 47);
  4. support women by facilitating and funding specific projects such as:
    (a) securing safe water supplies (cf. 48 a);
    (b) fostering indigenously-based self-help programmes (cf. 48 b);
    (c) educating women about their legal rights (cf. 48 c);
    (d) establishing programmes in congregations to study and implement the proposals of the WCC's Consultation on Sexism in the '70s as found in the report, "Discrimination Against Women," published in 1975;
    (e) supporting those organizations which are working to eliminate discrimination against women in political, economic, social, and ecclesial areas of life (cf. 47).
  77. Whereas we recognize the urgent need to examine ways in which women and men can grow into a partnership of mutual interdependence, *it is recommended that* the WCC urge its member churches to:
    1. affirm the personhood and mutual interdependence of individuals in families;
    2. affirm the personhood and worth of people living in different life situations (cf. 53);
    3. act upon these affirmations so as to enable women to realize their potential in every area of life;
    4. actively support programmes which investigate the exploitation of human sexuality for gain and seek to assist individuals who are exploited.
  78. Whereas these recommendations have such important implications for the Church, *it is further recommended that:*
    all member churches, especially their women's organizations, shall be urged to support women's concerns through special funds earmarked for the Women's Desk and to ask the WCC to appoint an additional staff member to co-ordinate the work.

ON HUMAN RIGHTS

Education and Conscientization on Human Rights

  79. The churches should:
    1. seek to raise Christian and public awareness of violations of human rights and their causes, developing educational materials for this purpose;
    2. educate their constituencies, particularly at congregational levels, to their rights and the legal recourses available to them;
    3. develop further technical expertise on human rights, perhaps through the creation of human rights institutes related to national and regional ecumenical bodies and providing scholarships for the study of human rights;
    4. in the light of the increasing incidence of torture and inhuman treatment of prisoners in many parts of the world, promote instruction on human rights and moral responsibility in the training of police and military personnel;
    5. include human rights in the formation of pastors, priests, and lay leaders, and in the curricula of other church training centres, such as development education institutions.

Information and Contacts

80. The churches should:

1. gather and disseminate information on different approaches to human rights, and on the basis of human rights;

2. gather reliable information on human rights violations in their own societies and elsewhere;

3. analyze such violations in order to discover their causes, reminding their constituencies regularly of how specific injustices reflect unjust social structures and seeking to avoid complicity with them;

4. develop effective channels of communication with one another, through personal contacts or otherwise, in order to ensure reliability of information and real effectiveness of active expressions of solidarity;

5. recognize, as a priority, that in the Middle East the rights of the Palestinian people under occupation should be implemented and work towards that end;

6. where the rights of entire peoples are violated through colonial domination; undue political, economic, or military interference in their national affairs; occupation of their lands by foreign powers; expulsion from their homelands; self-imposed racist, military, or other oppressive regimes—look beyond the propaganda of the offending power to the realities of those who suffer and help Christians and others to understand the true nature of their plight and struggles for their just rights. In co-operation with regional ecumenical bodies, the WCC should assist the churches in this task.

Legal Machinery for the Protection of Human Rights

81. The churches should:

1. help create new, improve existing, and facilitate access to legal institutions for the defence and promotion of human rights at community, national, and international levels;

2. seek access to prisons, camps, and other places of detention in order to obtain complete and accurate information about the treatment of inmates and conditions of detention, and defend the prisoners' rights to regular contact with family, friends, and legal counsel.

Action at Local, National, and Regional Levels

3. The struggle of the people themselves for their own rights is fundamentally important. Local congregations should become more active in identifying, documenting, and combating violations of human rights in their own communities. They and their national churches should seek ways to support the struggles of peoples, groups, and individuals for their own legitimate rights, helping them to form networks of solidarity to strengthen one another in their struggles.

4. Particular attention should be given to the special needs of political prisoners and refugees. In some cases, pastoral care becomes an act of courage, yet Christ calls us to minister both materially and spiritually to those in prison and to the outcasts as well as to their families.

5. Many changes are taking place in Asian governments. There is martial law in Taiwan; crisis government in the Philippines; emergency rule in India and South Korea; military rule in Bangladesh; one-party states in such countries as the People's Republic of China. In all other countries of Asia (e.g. Malaysia, Singapore, Australia, New Zealand, Indonesia, Japan) there are also violations of human rights. Wherever human rights are suppressed or violated by any Asian government, churches have a duty to work for the defence of human rights, especially of the oppressed. We believe the whole question of the mission of the Church is involved in this issue and urge churches to work for the rights of the people of Asia to participate in their own development.

6. Regional ecumenical bodies should help their churches to become more active in responding to the human rights needs of their societies. Work like that of the Christian Conference of Asia, and the consultation on "Human Rights and the Churches in Africa," sponsored by the All Africa Conference of Churches in collaboration with CCIA should be encouraged and pursued, and work like that of the interpretation programme of the MECC.

7. The report of the consultation on "Human Rights and Christian Responsibility" is commended to the churches for appropriate study and action (St Pölten, Austria, October 1974).

Responsibility of the WCC

82. The WCC should:

1. aid the churches in the above tasks;

2. gather and disseminate information about human rights violations within the limits of its possibilities;

3. help strengthen church leaders and Christians to perform the difficult tasks which face them, and to execute conscientiously their prophetic role in the face of abuses of power and inhuman practices in their churches, communities, and national societies;

4. provide a place for mutual challenge of the churches to become better servants; a place where the churches come together to give one another pastoral and material support as they become more courageously engaged in the struggle for human rights where they are; and a place to share strategies for struggle;

5. when necessary and appropriate, send pastoral and/or information-gathering teams to places where Christians and others are in need of support and encouragement in their own struggles for human rights;

6. use its consultative relationship with the UN, its possibilities to approach regional inter-governmental bodies and individual governments, and its co-operation with other non-governmental organizations in efforts to bring an end to human rights violations;

7. directly or through the CCIA issue public statements on violations of nations', groups', or individuals' human rights where this could serve those directly affected and, through clarifying the issues involved, contribute to the elimination of the root causes of such violations;

8. aid, materially and otherwise, groups and individuals who, because of their efforts to act out their Christian faith in defending human rights and in struggling

for justice in their societies, have become the objects of harassment, repression, imprisonment, or persecution.

ON RACISM

83. We commend the Programme to Combat Racism to the member churches, and urge them to ensure that their members receive accurate information about the whole programme. We ask for further support of the Programme in terms of increased commitment, prayer, and finance, in order that the various aspects of the Programme, e.g. theological reflection, action-oriented research, information, Annual Project List and Special Fund, may be even more effective.

84. Of primary importance to the churches' involvement in the struggle against racism is theological reflection on racism and on methods of combating it. We therefore draw to the churches' attention the ongoing joint project of the Programme to Combat Racism and Faith and Order and its report on a recent consultation, "Racism in Theology and Theology against Racism" (WCC 1975). We also encourage the study and implementation of the report on "Violence, Non-violence, and the Struggle for Social Justice," commended to the member churches by the Central Committee (Geneva 1973).

85. We urge member churches to ensure, wherever possible, the active participation of representatives from minority and racially oppressed groups in decision-making concerning their welfare and well-being within the life of churches and of society.

86. We urge member churches to provide factual information, gained from the oppressed groups themselves, so that Christians can learn the extent of their involvement in structures that perpetuate racial injustice and have recourse to specific proposals for responsible ecumenical action.

87. South Africa, which highlights racism in its most blatant form, must retain high priority for the attention of the member churches. Apartheid is possible only with the support of a large number of Christians there. We urge member churches to identify with, and wherever possible initiate or activate, campaigns to halt arms traffic; to work for the withdrawal of investments and the ending of bank loans; to stop white migration. These issues have already been urged by the WCC and we recommend these for urgent action by the member churches. Their implementation would be an effective non-violent contribution to the struggle against racism.

88. Racism, as a world problem, however, also demands the churches' attention in other particular situations, including

(a) the plight of the Korean minority in Japan;

(b) the condition of the native peoples of North and South America;

(c) the situation of the aboriginal peoples of Australia and ethnic minorities in New Zealand;

(d) growing racism against black people and migrant workers in Europe.

89. Churches everywhere should beware that their commendable zeal for combating racism and other forms of ethnocentrism in distant lands should not lead to ignoring its manifestations in their midst.

90. In all this, churches should be making a conscious effort to be themselves models of non-racist communities.

APPENDIX E

Program to Combat Racism: Grants, 1970–1986

In its first seventeen years, the WCC's Program to Combat Racism gave $6,906,545 to more than a hundred organizations in some thirty countries. Approximately 70 per cent went to political groups in many countries seeking to overthrow the white regime in South Africa. The three chief recipients were the African National Congress (ANC), South West Africa People's Organization (SWAPO), and the Pan Africanist Congress of Azania (PAC). These grants are listed in Appendix F. No grants were made in 1972. This table shows the grant totals by year and region. The figures are drawn from official WCC records.

	Africa	Australia/ Asia	South America	North America	Europe	Total
1970	135,000	27,000	15,000	—	23,000	200,000
1971	130,000	5,000	25,000	30,000	10,000	200,000
1973	101,000	14,000	20,000	41,000	18,000	194,000
1974	322,000	14,000	25,000	49,000	40,000	450,000
1975	257,000	37,500	60,000	73,500	72,000	500,000
1976	275,045	37,500	38,000	106,000	103,500	560,045
1977	265,000	50,000	22,500	95,000	92,500	525,000
1978	180,000	62,000	15,000	90,000	87,500	434,500
1979	40,000	63,000	—	96,000	150,000	349,000
1980	350,000	82,000	10,000	176,500	157,000	775,500
1981	250,000	112,000	15,000	81,000	129,000	587,000
1982	210,000	82,500	20,000	88,000	89,000	489,500
1983	235,000	50,500	23,000	69,000	68,500	446,000
1984	200,000	66,000	—	78,000	56,000	400,000
1985	225,000	43,000	—	78,500	49,500	396,000
1986	226,000	33,000	5,000	84,500	51,500	400,000
	$3,401,045	779,000	293,500	1,236,000	1,197,000	6,906,545

Grants to the ANC, SWAPO, and PAC, 1970–1986

*Of the $6,906,545 given by the WCC's Program to Combat
Racism, $2,494,500 (or 36 per cent) went to three militant
political groups seeking to overthrow by force and subversion the
white regime in South Africa: the African National Congress
(ANC), the South West Africa People's Organization (SWAPO),
and the Pan Africanist Congress of Azania (PAC). There were no
grants to the three organizations in 1972 or 1979, perhaps
because of severe criticism of the Program at those times. The
figures below are from official WCC records.*

	ANC	*SWAPO*	*PAC*	*Total*
1970	10,000	5,000	—	15,000
1971	5,000	25,000	—	30,000
1973	2,500	20,000	2,500	25,000
1974	15,000	30,000	15,000	60,000
1975	45,000	83,500	45,000	173,500
1976	50,000	85,000	50,000	185,000
1977	25,000	125,000	25,000	175,000
1978	25,000	125,000	25,000	175,000
1980	150,000	200,000	—	350,000
1981	65,000	125,000	45,000	235,000
1982	65,000	100,000	45,000	210,000
1983	70,000	105,000	50,000	225,000
1984	70,000	100,000	30,000	200,000
1985	77,000	110,000	33,000	220,000
1986	80,000	110,000	26,000	216,000
	$754,500	1,348,500	391,500	2,494,500

Notes

Chapter One

1. David Gill, ed., *Gathered for Life: Official Report of the Sixth Assembly of the World Council of Churches, Vancouver, 1983* (Grand Rapids: Eerdmans, 1983), p. 7.
2. Claude Malhuret, "Report From Afghanistan," *Foreign Affairs*, Winter 1983–1984, p. 430. See also Roger Fenton and Maggie Gallagher, "Inside Afghanistan," *The New Republic*, August 29, 1983, p. 18.
3. Gill, *Gathered for Life*, pp. 161–62.
4. Ibid., pp. 157–58.
5. See Ernest W. Lefever, "Moralism and U.S. Foreign Policy," in *Ethics and World Politics* (Baltimore: Johns Hopkins University Press, 1972), pp. 1–20.
6. Gill, *Gathered for Life*, pp. 324–47.
7. Paul Ramsey, *Who Speaks for the Church?* (Nashville: Abingdon Press, 1967), pp. 137–57. See also Ernest W. Lefever, "Evanston on International Affairs," in *Christianity and Crisis*, November 29, 1954.
8. Ibid. See also Edward Norman, *Christianity and the World Order* (New York: Oxford University Press, 1979), p. 59.
9. Quoted in Ernest W. Lefever, "Church and Politics: The Protestant Debate," *The Reporter*, January 11, 1968, p. 42.

Chapter Two

1. See Ernest W. Lefever, "Evanston on International Affairs," *Christianity and Crisis*, November 29, 1954, pp. 158–60.
2. Imre Miklos, "Some Experience of the Policy Regarding Churches in the Hungarian People's Republic" (Paper delivered at the Ecumenical Center, Geneva, October 27, 1978), pp. 10–11, mimeographed.
3. World Council of Churches, Report of the Consultation on Militarism, *CCIA Background Information*, 1978, No. 2, p. 4.
4. WCC, Report of the Consultation on Militarism, *CCIA Background Information*, 1978, No. 2, p. 10.
5. *Ecumenical Press Service*, April 20, 1978.
6. See North Atlantic Treaty Organization, *Facts and Figures* (Brussels: North Atlantic Treaty Organization Information Service, 1981), p. 294, for the text of a communique issued on December 12, 1979, following a special meeting of NATO foreign and defense ministers. See also Ernest W. Lefever and E. Stephen Hunt, editors, *The Apocalyptic Premise: Nuclear Arms Debated* (Washington: Ethics and Public Policy Center, 1982), pp. 126–127.
7. *Ecumenical Press Service*, February 21, 1980.
8. WCC, *Justice and Service: Report of Subgroup Three, Committee on Unit II, Central Committee, Geneva, 1980*, p. 3.

9. J. A. Emerson Vermaat, report of WCC Central Committee meeting, Geneva, August 22, 1980.

10. WCC, *Reports of the Churches in International Affairs, 1979–1982* (Geneva: WCC, 1983), pp. 45–46.

11. Paul Albrecht and Ninan Koshy, eds., *Before It's Too Late: The Challenge of Nuclear Disarmament* (Geneva: WCC, 1983), p. 29.

12. Ibid., p. 32.

13. Ibid., pp. 8 and 31.

14. William Sloane Coffin, Jr., "It's a Sin to Build a Nuclear Weapon" (Sermon delivered in Amsterdam, Holland, November 22, 1981), p. 3, mimeographed.

15. WCC, *Reports of the Churches in International Affairs, 1979–1982* (Geneva: WCC, 1983), p. 55.

16. Document No. 25, WCC Central Committee, Geneva, 1982, pp. 3 and 19.

17. Dorothee Soelle, "Life in Its Fullness," in Document TH#-1, WCC Vancouver Assembly, 1983, pp. 6–7.

18. David Gill, ed., *Gathered for Life: Official Report of the Sixth Assembly of the World Council of Churches, Vancouver, 1983* (Grand Rapids: Eerdmans, 1983), p. 75.

19. Ibid., pp. 73–74.

20. Quoted in Ernest W. Lefever and E. Stephen Hunt, editors, *The Apocalyptic Premise: Nuclear Arms Debated* (Washington: Ethics and Public Policy Center, 1982), p. 337.

21. Gill, *Gathered for Life*, p. 74.

22. Ibid., p. 133.

23. WCC Central Committee, "Statement on Nuclear Disarmament," Geneva, January 16–24, 1987, Document No. 7-1, Revised, three pages.

24. See U.S. Department of Defense and U.S. Department of State, *Soviet Defense Programs,* October 1985; Hans Ruhle, "Gorbachev's 'Star Wars,' " *NATO Review,* August 1985; "Red Star Wars," *Wall Street Journal,* April 10, 1985; "Moscow's Bigger Star Wars Drive," *Wall Street Journal,* December 16, 1986; and Keith Payne, "The Soviet Union and Strategic Defense: The Failure and Future of Arms Control," *Orbis: A Journal of World Affairs,* Winter 1986.

25. *One World,* March 1987, p. 5.

Chapter Three

1. Juan Hernandez Pico, "The Experiment of Nicaragua's Revolutionary Christians," in Sergio Torres and John Eagleson, ed., *The Challenge of Basic Christian Communities* (New York: Orbis Books/Maryknoll, 1982), p. 69. On Christian participation in the Nicaraguan Revolution, see Gerhard Koberstein, ed., *Nicaragua: Revolution und Christlicher Glaube* (Frankfurt am Main: Verlag Otto Lembeck, 1982).

2. Michael Novak, *Will It Liberate?: Questions About Liberation Theology* (New York: Paulist Press, 1986), and Quentin L. Quade, editor, *The Pope and*

Revolution: John Paul II Confronts Liberation Theology (Washington: Ethics and Public Policy Center, 1982).

3. *Ecumenical Press Service,* August 21, 1979, p. 4.

4. Shirley Christian, *Nicaragua: Revolution in the Family* (New York: Random House, 1985), p. 281.

5. David Gill, ed., *Gathered for Life: Official Report of the Sixth Assembly of the World Council of Churches, Vancouver, 1983* (Grand Rapids: Eerdmans, 1983), pp. 159–60.

6. *Ecumenical Press Service,* September 25, 1981.

7. *International Herald Tribune,* July 11, 1984.

8. See *Nicaragua: The Human Rights Record* (London: Amnesty International, March 1986), p. 21.

9. J. A. Emerson Vermaat, interview of WCC General Secretary Emilio Castro, Geneva, July 12, 1984.

10. See Joshua Muravchik, "The Slow Road to Communism," in Mark Falcoff and Robert Royal, editors, *The Continuing Crisis: U.S. Policy in Central America and the Caribbean* (Washington: Ethics and Public Policy Center, 1987), pp. 351–52.

11. Gill, *Gathered for Life,* p. 159.

12. Malle Niilus, ed., *Miskitos: Nicaragua* (Geneva: World Council of Churches, 1984).

13. Gill, *Gathered for Life,* p. 160.

14. *One World,* October/November 1983, p. 5

15. *Ecumenical Press Service,* September 26–30, 1983.

16. *Ecumenical Review,* Vol. 36, No. 1, 1984, pp. 108–9.

17. J. A. Emerson Vermaat, account of WCC Central Committee press conference, Buenos Aires, July 30, 1985.

18. "Pastoral Letter to the People of the Churches of Central America," in *Ecumenical Review,* No. 4, October 1985, p. 500.

19. *Neues Deutschland* (East Berlin), August 10–11, 1985, p. 1.

20. Gill, *Gathered for Life,* p. 160.

21. Advertisement in *The Times* (London), March 14, 1980. The advertisement was placed by the People's Revolutionary Army (ERP) of El Salvador.

22. Gill, *Gathered for Life,* p. 158.

23. World Council of Churches, *Your Kingdom Come: Report on the World Conference on Mission and Evangelism, Melbourne, May 1980* (Geneva: WCC, 1980), p. 243.

24. Full text is in *Ecumenical Press Service,* January 1–10, 1983.

25. WCC, *Reports of the Churches in International Affairs, 1979–1982* (Geneva: WCC, 1983), p. 125.

26. WCC, *Reports of the Churches in International Affairs, 1970–1973* (Geneva: WCC, 1974), p. 211.

27. See *The Challenge to Democracy in Central America* (Washington: Department of State and Department of Defense, June 1986), especially pp. 19, 20, 23, 38, 40, and 45. The data in the text have been updated by consultation with public affairs officers in the State Department.

28. Armando Valladares, *Against All Hope* (New York: Knopf, 1986).

29. Quoted in Humberto Belli, *Breaking Faith: The Sandinista Revolution and Its Impact on Freedom and Christian Faith in Nicaragua* (Garden City, Michigan: Puebla Institute, 1985), p. 247.

30. *One World,* May 1980, p. 21.

31. Jeane Kirkpatrick, "Cuba's Crimes," *Washington Post,* March 28, 1987.

Chapter Four

1. Reported in World Council of Churches, *Minutes of Central Committee,* Geneva, August 14-22, 1980, p. 165.

2. World Council of Churches, *Minutes of Central Committee,* Toronto, 1950, p. 91.

3. William C. Fletcher, *Religion and Soviet Foreign Policy 1945-1970* (London: Oxford University Press, 1973), p. 117.

4. *Ecumenical Press Service,* August 29, 1968.

5. WCC, *Minutes,* Central Committee, 1980, Geneva, p. 166.

6. *Journal of the Moscow Patriarchate,* 1980, No. 5, p. 5.

7. J. A. Emerson Vermaat, notes on World Council of Churches' Conference on Mission and Evangelism, "Your Kingdom Come," Melbourne, Australia, May 12-25, 1980.

8. Ibid., May 23, 1980.

9. Ibid., May 24, 1980.

10. WCC, *Your Kingdom Come: Report on the World Conference on Mission and Evangelism, Melbourne, May 1980* (Geneva: WCC, 1980), p. 242.

11. Vermaat, notes on plenary debate, WCC Central Committee, Geneva, August 21, 1980.

12. Vermaat, interview with Dr. Philip Potter, WCC general secretary, Geneva, August 22, 1980.

13. U.S. Congress, House, Subcommittee on Oversight of the Permanent Select Committee on Intelligence, *Hearings on Soviet Covert Action,* 96th Congress, Second Session, February 6 and 19, 1980, pp. 59 and 79.

14. *Ecumenical Press Service,* September 4, 1980.

15. David Gill, ed., *Gathered for Life: Official Report of the Sixth Assembly of the World Council of Churches, Vancouver, 1983* (Grand Rapids: Eerdmans, 1983), p. 161.

16. Document No. 2-11, WCC Sixth Assembly, Vancouver, 1983, p. 10.

17. *Canvas,* daily newspaper of the WCC, Vancouver, 1983, August 9, 1983, p. 2.

18. Gill, *Gathered for Life,* p. 161.

19. Ibid.

Chapter Five

1. Ernest W. Lefever, *Amsterdam to Nairobi: The World Council of Churches and the Third World* (Washington: Ethics and Public Policy Center, 1979), pp. 31-32.

2. Ibid., pp. 31-36.

3. World Council of Churches, *Programme to Combat Racism: Special Fund to Combat Racism,* annual reports of grants approved by the WCC's Executive Committee, 1970–1986.

4. WCC, *Report of the World Consultation on Racism, Churches Responding to Racism in the 1980s* (Geneva: WCC, 1980), p. 80.

5. Document No. 17, WCC Central Committee, Jamaica, 1979, p. 2. See also, WCC Central Committee, *Minutes and Reports of Nottingham Meeting, 1969,* p. 272.

6. See "ANC Admits It Gets Soviet Military Aid," *Washington Times,* June 5, 1987, p. 4.

7. *Trouw* (weekly paper), Amsterdam, August 1978.

8. *Newsweek* (International Edition), July 3, 1978, p. 15; *Algemeen Dagblad* (Rotterdam), June 26, 1978. See also Lefever, *Amsterdam to Nairobi,* p. 34.

9. *Ecumenical Press Service,* February 10, 1977.

10. *Newsweek* (International Edition), September 18, 1978, p. 23.

11. Ibid., p. 24.

12. WCC, *Minutes,* Central Committee, Kingston, Jamaica, 1–11 January 1979 (Geneva: WCC, 1979), p. 56.

13. *Ecumenical Review,* Vol. 31, No. 2, April 1979, p. 201.

14. Document No. 44A, WCC Central Committee, Jamaica, 1979, pp. 1–2.

15. *Ecumenical Press Service,* September 3, 1981.

16. Philip Potter and Archbishop Edward Scott, "Letter to Salvation Army," in *Ecumenical Press Service,* September 3, 1981.

17. *Ecumenical Press Service,* March 27, 1980, p. 2

18. Document No. 23, WCC Central Committee, Geneva, 1980, p. 10.

19. *Ecumenical Press Service,* February 28–March 6, 1982, item 82.03.09.

20. *One World,* July/August 1983, p. 5.

21. *Newsweek* (International Edition), May 7, 1984, p. 21.

22. *Ecumenical Press Service,* November 21–30, 1983, item 83.11.72.

23. J. A. Emerson Vermaat, account of remarks by Ninan Koshy at WCC press conference, Geneva, July 11, 1984.

24. *Washington Times,* May 25, 1987.

25. *Sunday Telegraph* (London), April 12, 1987. See also *Washington Times,* April 14, April 15, and May 1, 1987.

26. WCC, *Minutes,* Central Committee, Jamaica, January 1979, pp. 73–77.

27. WCC, *Minutes,* Central Committee, Dresden, German Democratic Republic, 1981, pp. 89–90.

28. David Gill, ed., *Gathered for Life: Official Report of the Sixth Assembly of the World Council of Churches, Vancouver, 1983* (Grand Rapids: Eerdmans, 1983), pp. 152–56.

29. For a discussion of the WCC's views on political violence, see Thomas S. Derr, *Barriers to Ecumenism* (Maryknoll, N.Y.: Orbis Books, 1983), pp. 52–58.

30. WCC, *Minutes,* Central Committee, Geneva, 1984, pp. 33–36.

31. WCC, *Minutes,* Central Committee, Buenos Aires, 1985, pp. 25–27.

32. See Richard E. Sincere, Jr., *The Politics of Sentiment: Churches and*

Foreign Investment in South Africa (Washington: Ethics and Public Policy Center, 1984).

33. Ibid., p. v, quoted from the *Johannesburg Sunday Times*, October 21, 1984.

34. Document 7-2, WCC Central Committee, Geneva, January 1987, five pages.

35. The quotations and other information on the Lusaka conference are drawn from a long page-one article, "Use of Force Against Apartheid Justified, Churches Contend," in the *National Catholic Register*, May 22, 1987.

Chapter Six

1. See Paul Seabury, *America's Stake in the Pacific* (Washington: Ethics and Public Policy Center, 1981).

2. David Gill, ed., *Gathered for Life: Official Report of the Sixth Assembly of the World Council of Churches, Vancouver, 1983* (Grand Rapids: Eerdmans, 1983), pp. 163 and 166.

3. Werner Schilling, "Das Raetsel der Oekumenischen Mao-Begeisterung," in W. Kuenneth and P. Beyerhaus, editors, *Reisch Gottes oder Weltgemeinschaft?* (Bad Liebenzell: Verlag der Liebenzeller Mission, 1975), pp. 155–56.

4. Dirk Bergvelt and Charlotte van Rappart, editors, *De Papieren Lente: Documenten van de Chinese Democratische Beweging, 1978–1980* (Utrecht and Antwepen: Het Spectrum, 1982), pp. 81 and 134.

5. World Council of Churches, *Reports of the Churches in International Affairs, 1979–1982* (Geneva: WCC, 1983), p. 107.

6. Ibid., p. 108. Also, *Ecumenical Press Service*, May 29, 1980, and *One World*, July 1980, p. 14.

7. Leopoldo Niilus, in the Introduction to "Human Rights in the Republic of Korea," in WCC, *CCIA Background Information*, No. 1, 1979, p. 2.

8. *Ecumenical Press Service*, September 22, 1977.

9. WCC, *Reports of the Churches in International Affairs, 1979–1982* (Geneva: WCC, 1983), p. 106.

10. Leopoldo Niilus, in the Introduction to "Iron Hand, Velvet Glove," in WCC, *CCIA Background Information*, No. 2, 1980, p. 2.

11. Gill, *Gathered for Life*, p. 166.

12. WCC, *Reports of the Churches in International Affairs, 1970–1973* (Geneva: WCC, 1974), p. 175.

13. Ibid., p. 179.

14. WCC, *Reports of the Churches in International Affairs, 1974–1978* (Geneva: WCC, 1979), p. 152.

15. *Europa van Morgen* (weekly information bulletin), The Hague, March 2, 1983, p. 151. See also *Washington Times*, April 3, 1987.

16. *U.S. News and World Report*, November 27, 1978; *Newsweek*, June 18 and July 2, 1979; *Time*, December 11, 1979.

17. David B. Barratt, ed., *World Christian Encyclopedia* (New York: Oxford

University Press, 1982), p. 746; *Religion in Communist Lands*, 1982, No. 1, p. 54.

18. *NRC Handelsblad* (Rotterdam), September 22, 1976; *Nederlands Dagblad* (Amersfoort, The Netherlands), September 23, 1976.

19. *Ecumenical Press Service*, June 9, 1977, p. 10.

20. David M. Paton, *Breaking Barriers: Official Report of the Fifth Assembly, World Council of Churches, Nairobi, 1975* (Grand Rapids: Eerdmans, 1976), p. 98.

21. Ibid., pp. 100 and 117.

22. WCC, *Minutes and Report of the 1973 Bangkok Assembly of the Commission on World Mission and Evangelism* (Geneva: WCC, 1973), p. 90; *International Review of Missions*, Vol. 62, No. 246, 1973, p. 181.

23. Philip Potter, press conference, Geneva, August 9, 1976, as reported by J. A. Emerson Vermaat.

24. Erich Weingartner, "Human Rights on the Ecumenical Agenda," in WCC, *CCIA Background Information*, No. 3, 1983, pp. 31 and 40.

25. WCC, *Reports of the Churches in International Affairs, 1979–1982* (Geneva: WCC, 1983), p. 100.

26. *Ecumenical Press Service*, June 21, 1979, p. 8.

27. *Ecumenical Press Service*, May 8, 1980, p. 4.

28. *Washington Times*, April 3, 1987.

Chapter Seven

1. David Gill, ed., *Gathered for Life: Official Report of the Sixth Assembly of the World Council of Churches, Vancouver, 1983* (Grand Rapids: Eerdmans, 1983), pp. 85–86.

2. Ibid., p. 88.

3. WCC, *Minutes*, Central Committee, Geneva, 1977 (Geneva: WCC, 1977), p. 44.

4. Ibid.

5. Gill, *Gathered for Life*, p. 86.

6. WCC, *Transnational Corporations, the Churches, and the Ecumenical Movement: Report of the WCC International Consultation on Transnational Corporations, Bad Boll, West Germany, 1981* (Geneva: WCC, 1982), p. 1.

7. David M. Paton, ed., *Breaking Barriers: Nairobi 1975* (Grand Rapids: Eerdmans, 1976), p. 131.

8. For further analyses of the WCC's position on South Africa, see Richard E. Sincere, Jr., *The Politics of Sentiment* (Washington: Ethics and Public Policy Center, 1984), and Thomas Oden, *Conscience and Dividends: Churches and the Multinationals* (Washington: Ethics and Public Policy Center, 1985).

9. WCC, *Minutes*, Central Committee Meeting, Geneva, 1977 (Geneva: WCC, 1977), p. 48.

10. Isaiah Frank, *Foreign Enterprise in Developing Countries* (Baltimore: Johns Hopkins University, 1980), p. 8.

11. WCC, *Minutes*, Central Committee Meeting, Geneva, 1977 (Geneva: WCC, 1977), p. 32.

12. WCC, *Minutes,* Central Committee Meeting, Geneva, 1982 (Geneva: WCC, 1982), p. 18.

13. Fidel Castro, address to the Third Congress of the Communist Party of Cuba, February 4, 1986, as translated by the U.S. Foreign Broadcast Information Service.

14. WCC, *Minutes,* Central Committee Meeting, Geneva, 1977 (Geneva: WCC, 1977), p. 44.

15. Ibid., p.43.

16. See "Socialism a la the World Council," in *Religion and Democracy,* newsletter of the Institute on Religion and Democracy, Washington, D.C., August 1983, p. 5.

17. For critiques of the NIEO and dependency theory, see Peter Bauer and B. S. Yamey, "Against the New Economic Order," in *Commentary* (April 1977), pp. 25–31; David B. H. Denoon, editor, *The New International Economic Order: A U.S. Response* (New York: New York University Press, 1979); P. T. Bauer, *Western Guilt and Third World Poverty* (Washington: Ethics and Public Policy Center, 1976); and Michael Novak, *Why Latin America Is Poor* (Washington: Ethics and Public Policy Center, 1982).

18. Presbyterian Task Force, *Review of Policies, Strategies, and Programs of the United Presbyterian Church Related to Transnational Corporations: Narrative Summary* (New York: General Assembly Mission Council, United Presbyterian Church, 1983), pp. 135–36 and general conclusions.

19. WCC, *Minutes,* Central Committee Meeting, Geneva, 1984 (Geneva: WCC, 1984), p. 44.

20. Ibid., pp. 56–57.

21. WCC, *Minutes,* Central Committee Meeting, Buenos Aires, 1985 (Geneva: WCC, 1985), p. 34.

22. Ibid., pp. 31–33.

23. WCC, *One World: The WCC 1986 Annual Report* (Geneva: WCC, 1987), p. 32.

24. Ibid.

25. "He Could Have Simply Crossed His Arms," report of the meeting on Confessing Movements and Economic Justice, Sao Paulo, Brazil, March 5–12, 1987 (sponsored by the WCC Commission on the Churches' Participation in Development and the Lutheran World Federation), p. 12.

26. Ibid., p. 14.

27. Activity Report No. 13, WCC Commission on the Churches' Participation in Development, Geneva, 1986, p. 3. For a summary of the WCC's views on economic questions from 1948 through the early 1980s, see Thomas Siegler Derr, "The Economic Thought of the World Council of Churches," *This World,* Winter-Spring 1982 (No. 1), pp. 14–27.

Chapter Eight

1. These other reliable groups include the Christian Rescue Effort for the Emancipation of Dissidents (CREED), the Research Center for Religious and

Human Rights in Closed Societies, publishers of *Religion in Communist Dominated Areas,* and the Slavic Gospel Association.

2. *Target,* daily newspaper of the Fifth Assembly of the World Council of Churches, Nairobi, Kenya, November 25, 1975, p. 4.

3. David M. Paton, ed., *Breaking Barriers: Nairobi 1975* (Grand Rapids: Eerdmans, 1976), p. 169.

4. Ibid.

5. J. A. Emerson Vermaat, notes of plenary debate of the Nairobi Assembly, December 9, 1975.

6. See J. A. Hebly, *The Russians and the World Council of Churches* (Belfast: Christian Journals, Ltd., 1978), pp. 73–77, 109–12, 121–23, 141, and 153. Hebly has written of Nikodim that he "is of the opinion that the present world with its antithesis between Communism and capitalism cannot be changed into 'an arena of idyllic mutual relations between fully reconciled classes, between have's and have not's, between oppressor and oppressed.' The ideological confrontation, which must be continued, is based on the reality of fundamentally different social-economic structures. . . . But we must choose for the ethical ideals of Communism as the best way. . . . Nikodim suggest[s] that Communism is light and capitalism darkness. The two systems are exclusive—one is right and the other wrong." See p. 153 of his book.

7. Paton, *Breaking Barriers,* p. 172.

8. World Council of Churches, "Montreux Memorandum," in "The Churches and Religious Liberty in the Helsinki Signatory States," in *CCIA Newsletter,* 1976, No. 4, p. 17.

9. Ibid., p. 20.

10. Document No. 6, WCC Central Committee, Geneva, 1976, p. 6.

11. *Ecumenical Press Service,* May 18, 1972.

12. *Washington Times,* May 28, 1987. See also *New York Times,* June 21, 1987.

13. WCC, "Study Paper on Religious Liberty," in *CCIA Background Information,* 1980, No. 4; see also WCC, *Minutes,* Central Committee, Geneva, 1980, p. 63.

14. See J. A. Hebly, *Church Times* (London), August 29, 1980, September 5, 1980, and September 12, 1980.

15. Full text in *Ecumenical Press Service,* October 30, 1980, pp. 3–4. See also *Ecumenical Press Service,* October 2, 1980, p. 2.

16. Full text in *Ecumenical Press Service,* November 13, 1980, pp. 8–9.

17. *One World,* July 1981, p. 19.

18. John Bluck, director of communications for the World Council of Churches, as quoted in *Ecumenical Press Service,* June 6–10, 1983, item 83.06.43.

19. J. A. Emerson Vermaat, record of a press conference by Ninan Koshy at Vancouver, August 8, 1983.

20. Translated from the Russian by Keston College, Kent, England, August 2, 1983. The German text is in *Glaube in der Zweiten Welt* (Zurich, 1983), No. 11, pp. 19–20.

21. WCC, *Reports of the Churches in International Affairs, 1979–1982* (Geneva: WCC, 1983), p. 107.

22. David Gill, ed., *Gathered for Life: Official Report of the Sixth Assembly of the World Council of Churches, Vancouver, 1983* (Grand Rapids: Eerdmans, 1983), p. 142.

23. Ibid., p. 140.

Chapter Nine

1. See J. A. Emerson Vermaat, "Moscow and the European Peace Movement," in *Problems of Communism,* November–December, 1982, reprinted by the Ethics and Public Policy Center, Washington, D.C., 1983. See also John Barron, "The KGB's Magical War for 'Peace,' " and Vladimir Bukovsky, "The Soviet Role in the Peace Movement," in Ernest W. Lefever and E. Stephen Hunt, editors, *The Apocalyptic Premise: Nuclear Arms Debated* (Washington: Ethics and Public Policy Center, 1982), pp. 111–38 and pp. 165–204.

2. Document No. 17, World Council of Churches Central Committee, Jamaica, 1979, p. 2. This was a background paper on southern Africa. See also World Council of Churches, *Minutes and Reports of the Central Committee, Nottingham, 1969,* p. 272.

3. For detailed information on WCC support of SWAPO and the ANC before 1979, see Ernest W. Lefever, *Amsterdam to Nairobi: The World Council of Churches and the Third World* (Washington: Ethics and Public Policy Center, 1979), pp. 30–38 and 92. Detailed information on WCC support of SWAPO and the ANC since 1979 is available from the WCC, Programme to Combat Racism, "Special Fund to Combat Racism," reports compiled annually, 1979–1985.

Chapter Ten

1. See Roy Godson, *Dezinformatsia: Active Measures in Soviet Strategy* (Pergamon Press, 1984). See also Roy Godson, editor, *Soviet Active Measures and Disinformation Forecast,* a quarterly newsletter published in Washington, D.C., and" 'Star Wars' Tops the Hit List of Soviet Propaganda Czars," *Washington Times,* February 9, 1987.

2. See Ernest W. Lefever, *Amsterdam to Nairobi: The World Council of Churches and the Third World* (Washington: Ethics and Public Policy Center, 1979), p. 40.

3. See Quentin L. Quade, editor, *The Pope and Revolution: John Paul II Confronts Liberation Theology* (Washington: Ethics and Public Policy Center, 1982), a symposium that includes a major essay by Gustavo Gutierrez, a foremost proponent of liberation theology; Michael Novak, *Will It Liberate?: Questions About Liberation Theology* (New York: Paulist Press, 1986); and Paul E. Sigmund, "Whither Liberation Theology?: A Historical Evaluation," in *Crisis,* January 1987, pp. 5–14.

4. See Michael Novak, *The Spirit of Democratic Capitalism* (New York:

Simon and Schuster, 1982), and Peter Berger, *The Capitalist Revolution* (New York: Basic Books, 1986).

5. See Stanley Rothman and S. Robert Lichter, *Roots of Radicalism: Jews, Christians, and the New Left* (New York: Oxford University Press, 1982), and Jean-Francois Revel, *The Totalitarian Temptation* (New York: Penguin, 1978).

6. See Real Jean Isaac, *America the Enemy: Profile of a Revolutionary Think Tank* (Washington: Ethics and Public Policy Center, 1980), and Joshua Muravchik, "Think Tank of the Left," in *New York Times Magazine*, April 26, 1981, pp. 36–38.

7. See, for example, Richard Barnett, *The Giants: Russia and America* (New York: Touchstone Books, 1977), and Barnett, *Intervention and Revolution: America's Confrontation With Insurrection Movements Around the World* (New York: Meridian Books, 1968).

8. See Irving Kristol, "'Wills' America: A 'Sophisticate' Takes Revenge," in *Washington Times*, February 9, 1987.

9. See Richard H. S. Crossman, *The God That Failed* (New York: Harper and Row, 1949), and Aleksandr Solzhenitsyn, *The Gulag Archipelago* (New York: Harper and Row, 1978).

10. See Lefever, *Amsterdam to Nairobi,* inside dustjacket.

11. Ibid., p. ix.

12. Reinhold Niebuhr's thought underwent three stages: his early pacifist-socialist phase from 1920 to the mid-1930s; his classic phase, similar to contemporary neoconservativism, from the mid-1930s to the early 1960s; and a later phase that is not consistent with his classic period. This analysis is documented in Ernest W. Lefever, Review of *Reinhold Niebuhr: A Biography,* by Richard Wightman Fox, and *The Essential Reinhold Niebuhr: Selected Essays and Addresses,* edited by Robert McAfee Brown, in *The American Spectator,* April 1986.

Epilogue

1. See transcript of "Sixty Minutes" program, "The Gospel According to Whom?," broadcast by the Columbia Broadcasting System (CBS-TV), head-quartered in New York City, on January 23, 1983. See also Rael Jean Isaac, "Do You Know Where Your Church Offerings Go?," in *Reader's Digest,* January 1983, pp. 120–25. See also *A Time for Candor: Mainline Churches and Radical Social Witness* (Washington: Institute on Religion and Democracy), December 1983.

2. Conversation with author, June 13, 1987.

3. Ernest W. Lefever, *Amsterdam to Nairobi: The World Council of Churches and the Third World* (Washington: Ethics and Public Policy Center, 1979), pp. 55–61.

4. Ibid., p. 56.

5. Ibid., p. 25.

6. Paul Ramsey, *Who Speaks for the Church?* (Nashville: Abingdon Press, 1967), pp. 15–16.

7. See Richard John Neuhaus, *The Naked Public Square* (Grand Rapids:

Eerdmans, 1984), especially pp. 220–22, and 245–47. For a Catholic perspective, see George Weigel, "Evangelicals and Catholics: A New Ecumenism?" in Richard John Neuhaus and Michael Cromartie, eds., *Piety and Politics: Evangelicals and Fundamentalists Confront the World* (Washington: Ethics and Public Policy Center, 1987), chapter 23. For classic interpretations of the relation of religion to the world, see H. Richard Niebuhr, *Christ and Culture* (New York: Harper and Row, 1951), and Reinhold Niebuhr, *Faith and History* (New York: Scribner's, 1949).

Bibliography

The titles below provide further background on the WCC and the issues addressed in this book. They are organized as follows:
- A. Official WCC Publications
- B. Appraisals of the WCC and the Ecumenical Movement
- C. The Catholic Church and Public Policy
- D. General Sources on International Issues
    1. Ethics and World Politics
    2. Nuclear Arms
    3. Central America
    4. Afghanistan
    5. Southern Africa
    6. East Asia and the Pacific
    7. The Economic Question
    8. Religion in the Soviet Bloc

A. Official WCC Publications

Albrecht, Paul, ed. *Faith, Science, and the Future*. Philadelphia: Fortress Press, with the World Council of Churches, 1978.

The Churches in International Affairs. Reports of the WCC Commission on Churches in International Affairs, 1970–73. Geneva: World Council of Churches, 1974.

Derr, Thomas Sieger. *Barriers to Ecumenism: The Holy See and the World Council on Social Questions*. New York: Orbis Books, 1983.

Evanston to New Delhi. Geneva: World Council of Churches, 1961.

Faith and Science in an Unjust World: Report of the WCC's Conference on Faith, Science, and the Future. Volume 1—Plenary Presentations, Roger L. Shinn, ed.; Volume 2—Reports and Recommendations, Paul Albrecht, ed. Geneva: World Council of Churches, 1980.

Gill, David. *From Here to Where? Technology, Faith, and the Future of Man*. Geneva: World Council of Churches, 1970.

———, ed. *Gathered for Life: Official Report of the Sixth Assembly of the World Council of Churches, Vancouver, Canada*. Grand Rapids: William B. Eerdmans, 1983.

Goodall, Norman, ed. *The Uppsala Report 1968*. Geneva: World Council of Churches, 1968.

Man's Disorder and God's Design. The Amsterdam Assembly Series of the WCC. New York: Harper and Brothers, 1948.

Minutes of the Annual Meetings of the Central Committee, World Council of Churches, 1975–1985.

Mosley, J. Brooke. *Christians in the Technical and Social Revolutions of Our Time*. Cincinnati: Forward Movement Press, 1966.

The Nature of the Church and the Role of Theology. Geneva: World Council of Churches, 1976.

The New Delhi Report: The Third Assembly of the World Council of Churches, 1961. New York: Association Press, 1962.

Northcott, Cecil. *Evanston World Assembly: A Concise Interpretation*. London: Lutterworth Press, 1954.

Official Report: World Conference on Church and Society. Philadelphia: Westminster Press, 1974.

One World: Annual Report of the World Council of Churches, 1987.

Paton, David M., ed. *Breaking Barriers: Nairobi 1975*. Grand Rapids: William B. Eerdmans, 1976.

Peace and Disarmament: Documents of the World Council of Churches and the Roman Catholic Church. Geneva and Rome: World Council of Churches and Catholic Pontifical Commission, 1982.

The Ten Formative Years 1938–1948. Geneva: World Council of Churches, 1948.

To Break the Chains of Oppression: Results of an Ecumenical Study Process on Domination and Dependence. Geneva: World Council of Churches, 1975.

Traitler, Reinhild. *In Search of the New (III)*. Geneva: World Council of Churches, 1981.

W. A. Visser 't Hooft, ed. *The First Assembly of the World Council of Churches*. New York: Harper and Brothers, 1949.

———. *The Evanston Report*. New York: Harper and Brothers, 1955.

World Conference on Church and Society: Geneva, July 12–26, 1966. Official Report, prepared by M. M. Thomas and Paul Albrecht. Geneva: World Council of Churches, 1967.

B. Appraisals of the WCC and the Ecumenical Movement

Austin, George. "The World Council of Churches' Programme to Combat Racism." *Conflict Studies* No. 105. London: Institute for the Study of Conflict, March 1979.

Bock, Paul. *In Search of a Responsible World Society: The Social Teachings of the World Council of Churches*. Philadelphia: Westminster Press, 1974.

Brown, Robert McAfee. *Theology in a New Key: Responding to Liberation Themes*. Philadelphia: Westminster Press, 1978.

Derr, Thomas Sieger. "The Economic Thought of the World Council of Churches." *This World*, Winter–Spring 1982, pp. 14–27.

Duff, Edward, S.J. *The Social Thought of the World Council of Churches*. New York: Association Press, 1956.

Genet, Harry. "World Council of Churches: A Case of Indigestion." *Christianity Today*, February 2, 1979.

Hebly, J. A. *The Russians and the WCC.* Belfast, Northern Ireland: Christian Journals Limited, 1978.

Hopkins, Charles Howard. *The Rise of the Social Gospel in American Protestantism, 1865–1915.* New Haven: Yale University Press, 1940.

Hudson, Darril. *The Ecumenical Movement and World Affairs.* Washington: The National Press, 1969.

Lefever, Ernest W. *Amsterdam to Nairobi: The World Council of Churches and the Third World.* Washington: Ethics and Public Policy Center, 1979.

———. "Evanston and International Affairs." *Christianity and Crisis*, November 29, 1954.

May, Henry F. *Protestant Churches and Industrial America.* New York: Harper and Brothers, 1949.

Miller, Robert Moats. *American Protestantism and Social Issues, 1919–1939.* Chapel Hill: University of North Carolina Press, 1958.

Neuhaus, Richard John. *The Naked Public Square: Religion and Democracy in America.* Grand Rapids: William B. Eerdmans, 1984.

Nichols, James Hastings. *Evanston: An Interpretation.* New York: Harper and Brothers, 1954.

Norman, Edward. *Christianity and the World Order.* Oxford: Oxford University Press, 1979.

Ramsey, Paul. *Who Speaks for the Church?* Nashville: Abingdon Press, 1967.

C. The Catholic Church and Public Policy

Benestad, J. Brian. *The Pursuit of a Just Social Order: Policy Statements of the U.S. Catholic Bishops, 1966–80.* Washington: Ethics and Public Policy Center, 1982.

Carey, George, and James V. Schall, eds. *Essays in Christianity and Political Philosophy.* Lanham, Md.: University Press of America, 1984.

Novak, Michael. *Freedom with Justice.* San Francisco: Harper and Row, 1981.

———. *The Spirit of Democratic Capitalism.* New York: Simon & Schuster, 1982.

Quade, Quentin, L., ed. *The Pope and Revolution: John Paul II Confronts Liberation Theology.* Washington: Ethics and Public Policy Center, 1982.

Schall, James V., *Christianity and Politics.* Boston: Daughters of St. Paul, 1981.

Weigel, George. *Tranquillitas Ordinis: The Present Failure and Future Promise of American Catholic Thought on War and Peace.* New York: Oxford University Press, 1987.

D. General Sources on
International Issues

A number of periodicals devoted largely or entirely to international affairs contain frequent articles on the specific issues the WCC has addressed. Such periodicals include *Commentary, Foreign Affairs, Foreign Policy, Global Affairs, International Security, International Security Review, National Review, The New Republic, Orbis, Strategic Review, The Washington Quarterly,* and *World Policy Journal.* The International Institute for Strategic Studies (IISS) in London issues two very helpful annual publications, *The Military Balance* and *Strategic Survey. Foreign Affairs* annually publishes a "year in review" issue that provides an excellent survey of developments in international relations and U.S. foreign policy during the preceding year.

There are dozens of more specialized journals that focus on specific areas or issues dealt with in this book. For example, Asian affairs are covered in *Asian Survey,* the Pacific Defense Reporter, the *China Quarterly,* and many other magazines. Any major library, especially university libraries, should carry journals with a specific regional focus.

I. ETHICS AND WORLD POLITICS

Bennett, John C., and Harvey Seifert. *U.S. Foreign Policy and Christian Ethics.* Philadelphia: Westminster Press, 1977.

Fosdick, Dorothy. *Common Sense and World Affairs.* New York: Harcourt, Brace and Co., 1955.

Halle, Louis J. *Civilization and Foreign Policy.* New York: Harper and Brothers, 1955.

Herz, John H. *Political Realism and Political Idealism.* Chicago: University of Chicago Press, 1951.

Kennan, George F. *Realities of American Foreign Policy.* Princeton: Princeton University Press, 1954.

Kirkpatrick, Jeane J. *Dictatorships and Double Standards: Rationalism and Reason in Politics.* New York: Simon and Schuster, 1982.

Lefever, Ernest W. *Ethics and U.S. Foreign Policy.* Original edition, 1957. Reprinting, Lanham, Md.: University Press of America, 1986.

———, ed. *Ethics and World Politics: Four Perspectives.* Baltimore and London: The Johns Hopkins University Press, 1972.

———, ed. *Morality and Foreign Policy: A Symposium on President Carter's Stance.* Washington: Ethics and Public Policy Center, 1977.

Morgenthau, Hans J. *In Defense of the National Interest.* New York: Alfred A. Knopf, 1951.

Niebuhr, Reinhold. *Christianity and Power Politics.* New York: Charles Scribner's Sons, 1940.

Novak, Michael. *Moral Clarity in the Nuclear Age.* Nashville: Thomas Nelson Publishers, 1983.

Osgood, Robert E. *Ideals and Self-Interest in America's Foreign Relations.* Chicago: University of Chicago Press, 1953.
Pfaltzgraff, Robert L., Jr. *National Security: Ethics, Strategy, and Politics.* Washington: Pergamon-Brassey's for the Institute for Foreign Policy Analysis, 1986.
Weinberger, Caspar, and George Shultz. *Ethics and American Power.* Washington: Ethics and Public Policy Center, May 1985.

2. NUCLEAR ARMS

Brzezinski, Zbigniew, et al., eds. *Promise or Peril: The Strategic Defense Initiative.* Washington: Ethics and Public Policy Center, 1986.
English, Raymond, ed. *Ethics and Nuclear Arms: European and American Perspectives.* Washington: Ethics and Public Policy Center, 1985.
Freedman, Lawrence D. *The Evolution of Nuclear Strategy.* New York: St. Martin's Press, 1981.
Griffiths, Franklin, and John C. Polanyi, eds. *The Dangers of Nuclear War.* Toronto: University of Toronto Press, 1979.
Haley, P. Edward, et al., eds. *Nuclear Strategy, Arms Control, and the Future.* Boulder, Colo.: Westview Press, 1985.
The Harvard Nuclear Study Group. *Living With Nuclear Weapons.* New York: Bantam Books, 1983.
Kahn, Herman. *On Thermonuclear War.* Princeton: Princeton University Press, 1960.
———. *Thinking About the Unthinkable.* New York: Horizon Press, 1962.
Kegley, Charles W., Jr., and Eugene R. Wittkopf. *The Nuclear Reader: Strategy, Weapons, War.* New York: St. Martin's Press, 1985.
Kennan, George. *The Nuclear Delusion: Soviet-American Relations in the Nuclear Age.* New York: Pantheon Press, 1982.
Kissinger, Henry A. *Nuclear Weapons and Foreign Policy.* New York: Anchor Books, 1958.
Lefever, Ernest W., ed. *Arms and Arms Control.* New York: Praeger Publishers, 1962.
———, and E. Stephen Hunt, eds. *The Apocalyptic Premise: Nuclear Arms Debated.* Washington: Ethics and Public Policy Center, 1982.
Woolsey, R. James, ed. *Nuclear Arms: Ethics, Strategy, Politics.* San Francisco: Institute for Contemporary Studies, 1984.

3. CENTRAL AMERICA

Christian, Shirley. *Nicaragua: Revolution in the Family.* New York: Random House, 1985.
Erisman, H. Michael, and John D. Martz, eds. *Colossus Challenged: The Caribbean Struggle for Independence.* Boulder, Colo.: Westview Press, 1982.
Falcoff, Mark, and Robert Royal, eds. *The Continuing Crisis: U.S. Policy in*

Central America and the Caribbean. Washington: Ethics and Public Policy Center, 1987.

Gettleman, Marvin, et al., eds. *El Salvador: Central America in the New Cold War.* New York: Grove Press, 1981.

Leiken, Robert S. *Central America: Anatomy of Conflict.* Washington: Pergamon-Brassey's for the Carnegie Endowment for International Peace, 1984.

Levine, Barry, ed. *The New Cuban Presence in the Caribbean.* Boulder, Colo.: Westview Press, 1983.

Valenta, Jiri, and Herbert Ellison, eds. *Grenada and the Soviet/Cuban Policy: Internal Crisis and U.S./OECS Intervention.* Boulder, Colo.: Westview Press for the Kennan Institute for Advanced Russian Studies, 1986.

Wiarda, Howard J., ed. *Rift and Revolution: The Central American Imbroglio.* Washington: American Enterprise Institute, 1984.

Williams, Eric. *From Columbus to Castro: The History of the Caribbean, 1492–1969.* New York: Random House, 1983.

4. AFGHANISTAN

Arnold, Anthony. *Afghanistan: The Soviet Invasion in Perspective.* Stanford, Calif.: Hoover Institution Press, 1981.

Bradster, Henry S. *Afghanistan and the Soviet Union.* Durham, N.C.: Duke University Press, 1983.

Cronin, Richard P. *Afghanistan: Soviet Invasion and U.S. Response.* Washington: U.S. Library of Congress, Congressional Research Service, 1981.

Deniau, Jean-Francois. "Two Hours After Midnight: With the Mujahideen in Afghanistan." *Encounter,* September/October 1986.

Fenton, Roger, and Maggie Gallagher. "Inside Afghanistan." *The New Republic,* August 29, 1983.

Free Afghanistan Report. Committee For a Free Afghanistan, Washington, D.C.

Hammond, Thomas T. *Red Flag Over Afghanistan.* Boulder, Colo.: Westview Press, 1984.

Jones, Allan K. *Afghan Refugees: Five Years Later.* Washington: Committee for Refugees Issue Paper, January 1985.

Malhuret, Claude. "Report From Afghanistan." *Foreign Affairs,* Winter 1983/84.

Monks, Alfred L. *The Soviet Intervention in Afghanistan.* Washington: American Enterprise Institute, 1981.

United States Department of State. "Afghanistan: 18 Months of Occupation." Special Report No. 86, August 1981.

World Affairs, Winter 1982–1983. Special issue on Afghanistan.

5. SOUTHERN AFRICA

Bissell, Richard E. *South Africa and the United States: The Erosion of An Influence Relationship.* New York: Praeger Publishers, 1982.

Crocker, Chester A. "South Africa: Strategy for Change." *Foreign Affairs,* Winter 1980/81.

Gann, L. H., and Peter Duignan. *South Africa: War, Revolution, or Peace?* Stanford, Calif.: Hoover Institution Press, 1978.

Hanks, Robert J. *Southern Africa and Western Security.* Cambridge, Mass.: Institute for Foreign Policy Analysis, 1983.

Jaster, Robert S. *South Africa and Its Neighbors: The Dynamics of Regional Conflict.* Adelphi Papers No. 209. London: International Institute for Strategic Studies, Summer 1986.

Kitchen, Helen. *U.S. Interests in Africa.* The Washington Papers, 98. New York: Praeger Publishers, 1983.

———, and Michael Clough. *The United States and South Africa: Realities and Red Herrings.* Washington: Center for Strategic and International Studies, 1984.

Parker, Frank J. *South Africa: Lost Opportunities.* Lexington, Mass.: Lexington Books, 1983.

Sincere, Richard E., Jr. *The Politics of Sentiment: Churches and Foreign Investment in South Africa.* Washington: Ethics and Public Policy Center, 1984.

South Africa 1985: Official Yearbook of the Republic of South Africa. Johannesburg: Chris van Rensburg Publications, 1985.

Study Commission on U.S. Policy Toward South Africa. *South Africa: Time Running Out.* Berkeley: University of California Press, 1981.

6. EAST ASIA AND THE PACIFIC

Barnett, A. Doak. *China and the Major Powers in East Asia.* Washington: The Brookings Institution, 1977.

Clough, Ralph N. *Island China.* Cambridge, Mass.: Harvard University Press, 1978.

Gelb, Leslie, and Richard Betts. *The Irony of Vietnam.* Washington: The Brookings Institution, 1979.

Gregor, A. James. *Crisis in the Philippines.* Washington: Ethics and Public Policy Center, 1984.

———, and Virgilio Aganon. *The Philippine Bases: U.S. Security at Risk.* Washington: Ethics and Public Policy Center, 1987.

———, and Maria Hsia Chang. *The Iron Triangle: A U.S. Security Policy for Northeast Asia.* Stanford, Calif.: Hoover Institution Press, 1984.

———. *The Republic of China and U.S. Policy: A Study in Human Rights.* Washington: Ethics and Public Policy Center, 1983.

Jackson, Karl D., and Hadi Soesastro, eds. *ASEAN Security and Economic Development.* Berkeley, Calif.: Institute of East Asian Studies, 1984.

Lake, Anthony, ed. *The Legacy of Vietnam.* New York: New York University Press, 1976.

Palmer, Bruce, Jr. *The 25-Year War: America's Military Role in Vietnam.* New York: Simon and Schuster, 1984.

Podhoretz, Norman. *Why We Were in Vietnam.* New York: Simon and Schuster, 1982.

Seabury, Paul. *America's Stake in the Pacific.* Washington: Ethics and Public Policy Center, 1981.

Solomon, Richard H., and Masataka Kosaka, eds. *The Soviet Far East Military Buildup: Nuclear Dilemmas and Asian Security*. Dover, Mass.: Auburn House, 1986.

Tasker, Rodney. "The [Indochina] War Continues." *Far Eastern Economic Review*, May 9, 1985.

Zagoria, Donald S. *Soviet Policy in East Asia*. New Haven: Yale University Press, 1982.

7. THE ECONOMIC QUESTION

Amacher, Ryan C., Gottfried Haberler, and Thomas D. Willett, eds. *Challenges to a Liberal International Economic Order*. Washington: American Enterprise Institute, 1979.

Bauer, P. T. *Equality, the Third World, and Economic Delusion*. Cambridge, Mass.: Harvard University Press, 1981.

———, and B. S. Yamey. "Against the New Economic Order." *Commentary*, April 1977.

Bedjaoui, Mohammed. *Towards a New International Economic Order*. New York: Holmes and Meier for UNESCO, 1979.

Bhagwati, Jagdish N., ed. *The New International Economic Order: The North-South Debate*. Cambridge, Mass.: MIT Press, 1977.

Chamberlain, Neil. *The Limits of Corporate Responsibility*. New York: Basic Books, 1973.

DeGeorge, Richard, and Joseph A. Pichler, eds. *Ethics, Free Enterprise, and Public Policy: Original Essays on Moral Issues in Business*. New York: Oxford University Press, 1978.

Denoon, David B. H., ed. *The New International Economic Order: A U.S. Response*. New York: New York University Press, 1979.

Drucker, Peter. *Concept of the Corporation*. New York: John Day, 1972.

French, Peter A. "The Corporation as a Moral Person." *American Philosophical Quarterly*, July 1979.

Heilbroner, Robert L., et al. *In the Name of Profit: Profiles in Corporate Responsibility*. Garden City, N.Y.: Doubleday, 1972.

Manne, Henry G., and Henry C. Wallich. *The Modern Corporation and Social Responsibility*. Washington: American Enterprise Institute, 1972.

Oden, Thomas C. *Conscience and Dividends: Churches and the Multinationals*. Washington: Ethics and Public Policy Center, 1985.

Rubin, Seymour J. "Economic and Social Human Rights and the New International Economic Order." *The American University Journal of International Law and Policy*, Summer 1986.

Tucker, Robert W. *The Inequality of Nations*. New York: Basic Books, 1977.

8. RELIGION IN THE SOVIET BLOC

Bach, Markus. *God and the Soviets*. New York: Thomas Crowell Company, 1958.

Bociurkiw, Bohdan, R. "Soviet Religious Policy." *Problems of Communism*, May-June 1973.

Boiter, Albert. *Religion in the Soviet Union*. The Washington Papers, 78. Beverly Hills, Calif.: Sage Publications, 1980.

Conquest, Robert. *Religion in the USSR*. New York and Washington: Praeger Publishers, 1966.

Dunn, Dennis J., ed. *Religion and Modernization in the Soviet Union*. Boulder, Colo.: Westview Press, 1977.

Fletcher, William C., and Max Haywood, eds. *Religion and the Soviet State: A Dilemma of Power*. New York: Praeger Publishers, 1969.

Lowry, Charles W. *Communism and Christianity*. New York: Collier Books, 1962.

Religion in Communist Dominated Lands, a New York periodical.

Religion in Communist Lands, a London periodical.

Index of Names

DATE DUE
